Praise for
How I Found God in Everyone and Everywhere: Volume II:
A Futher Anthology of Spiritual Memoirs

"There is a mystic in every person waiting to be acknowledged. In this text, a baker's dozen of spiritual leaders tells the stories of their unique spiritual adventures. Their stories are authentic, honest, inspiring, and challenge the reader to embark on their own spiritual quest. This text reminds us that in this moment, right where we are, we can experience the Holy. We have everything we need to venture on the high seas of mystical adventure. The questions and suggestions that conclude each chapter make this book ideal for book groups." —**Bruce G. Epperly**, author of *The Elephant Is Running: Process and Open and Relational Theology and Religious Pluralism*

"This collection of spiritual memoirs offers no conclusions as to the "what" of the spiritual path. Instead, each chapter highlights the personal "how," "why," and "who" of ongoing spiritual adventures. Since the dogma is missing, this anthology is a terrific companion to diverse individuals and groups of spiritual seekers who may appreciate the company of a few fellow sojourners along the way." —**Rev. Bonnie Rambob**, pastor, public school teacher, writer, podcast co-host

"As a chaplain, I am witness to countless stories of spiritual journey. Each is unique and often they follow a winding road of arrivals and departures, each moment intertwining with the next. This anthology invites you into the inner sanctum of spiritual exploration, where leaders and seekers share their most intimate encounters with mystery. I share Andrew Davis' hope that discussion groups will form and participants will explore together. My wish for readers is that they find fellow seekers for exploration in community, a renewed sense of wonder, and the courage to tell their own story of spiritual becoming." —**Kathleen Reevs**, board certified chaplain

"Inspirational stories of people experiencing God are not limited to saints who lived long ago in a pre-scientific era of mysticism. Right here and right now, in our modern world, many continue to have surprising encounters with profound effects. This book testifies that experiencing God saturates and overflows our capacities, it remains an encounter that takes hold of us, transforms us, and helps us see the depth of beauty that we are all part of." —**Andre Rabe**, author of *Processing Memetic Reality*

"As the river refracts the sunlight, so one's story refracts the truth—a thousand different points of beauty. Given this anthology contains 13 stories, by my math, the reader must have access to at least 13,000 different points of beauty. From musicians to thinkers, philosophers to preachers, this is writing marked by a sense of spirit and truth." —**Jonathan J. Foster**, author of *indigo: the color of grief*

"Physicists, medical doctors, professors, clergy, founders of spiritual centers and schools, musicians, and artists recount their unexpected personal encounters convincing them that God exists. Study questions and recommended exercises follow each narrative. Form a small group of four to eight persons to read these sacred encounters—love stories, personal hymns of praise—and undertake the exercises together. Continue to meet after you have completed all of the exercises and you will have the spiritual community you longed for but didn't know how to create. This book is a marvelous and powerful work." —**The Rev. Dr. Thandeka**, Unitarian Universalist minister and theologian; founder of Affect Theology

"This rich, inspiring volume will serve its readers not only as food for thought, but for the spirit as well. Its first-person accounts of spiritual illumination draw from a variety of traditional and non-traditional

sources. It is a book that's highly appropriate to our times, which are characterized both by an ever-increasing diversity of worldviews, and an ever-increasing need for true inspiration and grounding in the Real."
—**Jeffery D. Long**, Carl W. Zeigler Professor of Religious Studies, Elizabethtown College

how I found GOD in everyone and everywhere

volume II

*A Further Anthology
of Spiritual Memoirs*

Andrew M. Davis

Monkfish Book Publishing Company
Rhinebeck, New York

Paperback ISBN 978-1-958972-43-4
eBook ISBN 978-1-958972-44-1

Library of Congress Cataloging-in-Publication Data

Names: Davis, Andrew M., 1987- editor. | Clayton, Philip, 1956- editor.
Title: How I found God in everyone and everywhere : an anthology of spiritual
   memoirs / [edited by] Andrew M. Davis & Philip Clayton.
Description: Rhinebeck, New York : Monkfish Book Publishing Company, 2018.
Identifiers: LCCN 2018010751 (print) | LCCN 2018010938 (ebook) | ISBN
   9781939681898 (ebook) | ISBN 9781939681881 (pbk. : alk. paper)
Subjects: LCSH: Pantheism. | Panentheism. | Spiritual biography.
Classification: LCC BL220 (ebook) | LCC BL220 .H69 2018 (print) | DDC
   204--dc23
LC record available at https://lccn.loc.gov/2018010751

Book and cover design by Colin Rolfe

Monkfish Book Publishing Company
22 East Market Street, Suite 304
Rhinebeck, New York 12572
USA (845) 876-4861
www.monkfishpublishing.com

For seekers, wanderers, and storytellers

"Physical wandering is still important, but greater still is the power of [our] spiritual adventures—adventures of thought, adventures of passionate feeling, adventures of aesthetic experience."

—*Alfred North Whitehead*

"A sense of the universe, a sense of the all, the nostalgia which seizes us when confronted by nature, beauty, music—these seem to be an expectation and awareness of a Great Presence."

—*Pierre Teilhard de Chardin*

Contents

Introduction: The Journey Continues...

Andrew M. Davis

It may seem that the spiritual journey can only be told in retrospect. But even from the place of its telling, you find yourself in its midst. It's not obvious that one ever fully "arrives" spiritually, religiously, or theologically, because as soon you think you "arrive," you often find yourself departing once more. To *arrive* anywhere, after all, is to have *departed* from somewhere else. The spiritual journey certainly has its pitstops, flip-flops, and round-abouts, but it never really stops—and that's a good thing. Like the universe itself, the spiritual journey is a continual process of discovery.

I've come to see that spiritual arrival is just as important as spiritual departure, and that these are intimately tangled in the ongoing journeys of our lives. Yet even in the flux of our spiritual journeys, we find something that abides with us. It may be a profound experience, a teacher, a school of thought, a practice, or an idea that keeps forming and re-forming as our journey continues. For many people, the idea of "God" is kind of like that.

The idea of God is not settled any more than the universe itself; nor, in principle, can it ever be. "God" is not a proper name, but a pointer to what Karl Rahner called the "Holy Mystery" at the heart of existence.

What we can say of the experience and reality of this Holy Mystery is perhaps little; words will inevitably fall short. This too is a good thing. You may have noticed, however, that we are hardly content to remain silent on such matters—even if silence is the most appropriate response. We want to speak of, about, and to this Holy Mystery, locating its presence or absence among the unfolding chapters of our life story. We remain deeply *narrative* beings—and narratives require *narration*.

For a number of years now, I've nurtured an interest in who or what God has come to mean for individuals who are navigating the various landscapes of the spiritual journey. Mind you, not just any individuals, but those who are recognized leaders, teachers, and practitioners across philosophy, theology, science, and religion. I've not only been interested in *what* these leaders affirm about God, but more so, in *how* they've come to these affirmations: the existential ups and downs, the sudden intellectual turns, the profound mystical experiences, and novel theological discoveries that form (and inform) the spiraling DNA of their personal spiritual narratives.

My 2018 volume with Philip Clayton titled, *How I Found God in Everyone and Everywhere: An Anthology of Spiritual Memoirs*, collected the personal spiritual narratives of key leaders in order to showcase the diversities and resonances of their experiences, including a discovery of a far more inclusive and immanent understanding of God—what some call *panentheism* (meaning, in Greek, "All-in-God"). In ways I could not initially foresee, this book became a resource not only for individuals walking the spiritual path, but for a variety of congregations, communities, and groups who were committed to walking this path *together*. I received many messages that the book was being read, studied, and discussed in such settings for the wisdom and possibilities it affords for continuing the spiritual journey and affirming (or re-affirming) the reality of God as immanent, experiential, and all-encompassing.

Some months after its publication, I was a bit uneasy. Two realizations struck me. The first concerned the inexhaustibility of spiritual narratives as an opportunity: *There's no end to the collection of spiritual memoirs by seasoned leaders and seekers*, I thought, followed by, *This should be the first in a series of books.* The second was a thought of regret: *I wish I was more deliberate in catering the book to group study and engagement.*

Both of these thoughts are now actualized in the book before you. This book is the second volume in my emerging "Anthology of Spiritual Memoir Series" with Monkfish. Like the first volume, it collects the personally written spiritual and intellectual narratives of pioneering minds. These memoirs are adventurous, inspiring, and even deeply challenging. From dark nights of suffering and despair, to the joy of scientific and intellectual discovery, to the aesthetic beauty of music and nature, and the blissful and, at times, dreadful shock of psychedelic, mystical, and near-death experience, these memoirs reveal exceptional encounters with the Holy Mystery—a universal Mind that exceeds, but also includes, our own.

Unlike the first volume, this book anticipates group study with "Questions for Discussion" and "Sages to Explore" sections. The questions deliberately probe aspects of each chapter allowing you to reflect individually and also share collectively. The sages appear as influential spiritual guides in each chapter. My hope is that through engaging the discussion questions and investigating further the many sages, you and your community will be deepened.

The spiritual journey is interior to each one of us, but it is not meant to be walked alone. I've come to see that sharing personal spiritual narratives is an essential part of the journey itself. Spiritual narratives are *spiritual resources*; they are lifelines which can revive dormant and dying journeys into the freshness of adventure and zest. It's not only the case that in telling your own spiritual narrative, new depth dimensions can be revealed to you about who and what you are, but also that in closely attending to the paths of others, you begin to see who you might *still become.*

The spiritual journey is far from static and always begins again when we discover new insights and inspirations. As you read, I hope you will be enlightened as to the unfinished nature of the quest, with its many arrivals and departures, and the horizon of possibilities still ahead. May your understanding of the Holy Mystery of things be deepened, expanded, and transformed, and may you also begin telling the tale of your own spiritual becoming.

I: Via Feminina *and the Monk Within*

Beverly Lanzetta

My immersion in global contemplative consciousness began over forty-five years ago when a series of revelatory experiences changed my life and set me on a path of devotion. What I've learned over these years is that the spiritual quest is a fundamental orientation common to the human experience. The commitment to seek God, and the pursuit of liberation or union with the Absolute are imprinted on the heart of the world. I also have learned that we live in an era of new visions of the sacred; the monastic heart resides within all people, regardless of life situation or vocation; and it is a sacred duty to share contemporary spiritual ways of being in a world often lacking healthy models of faith.

Youth

I was a solitary child, often choosing to stay home when my parents and sister went out to dinner or to the movies. Alone I felt a Presence that inspired and comforted me in ways that were unavailable with family or with friends. This freedom of being was most apparent in nature, where I formed bonds of intimacy with stately oaks and white tail deer.

At five years old I had my first visionary experience. One evening when I was bedridden with the chicken pox, an immense figure of light as tall as the ceiling appeared in the corner of my room. A glowing, pulsating vibration that was wise and calm and protective expanded in the air the way helium fills a birthday balloon. Instantly, a sweet feeling of comfort filled my being. The Special One spoke: *You cannot die. You have work to do.* Since my imagination often was populated by spirit figures and intuitive insights, it never occurred to me that others did not see the world the same way.

I remember being a sensitive child, but also wary, and a bit traumatized by harsh behaviors and the sloppy manner in which society handled the most significant events. Cruelty among my classmates affected me deeply. Yelling, loud noises, and punishment was unbearable. I learned to withdraw, to pull deeper into silence, to avoid contact, to hide. In a way, I became a critic of the world, interiorized and mute. Unable to speak about my secret inner life, my confidence eroded.

In our home, religious life was palpable, if not conventional. My grandmother, with whom I shared a bedroom, taught me to pray, and took me to confession and Sunday mass. My parents were more Christmas Eve and Easter Sunday Catholics, critical of the restrictions placed on the faithful. Yet, spirit was always present. My mother reminded us to love God, to call upon the "White Light of the Holy Spirit," and to seek truth. She was open to the visionary and intuitive realms, including the gifts of spiritualists, psychics, and healers. My father, quieter and less effusive, once shared with me an event that shaped the moral compass of his life: as a young man, sitting in the back of the church, he saw an apparition of Jesus standing to the left of the altar pointing to him.

And while I attended Sunday School and was anointed by the rites of the Church, I have no recollection of praying to Jesus or to a male God. Even then, it seems that Holy Mystery defied naming.

Adulthood

Looking back, I recognize elements of the person I am today in that child. I see God working in me, imperceptibly guiding me to a different future.

Like many women of my generation, I pursued the path of marriage and children. I needed to sort out the spiritual implications of gender roles: marriage, motherhood, and sexism. I needed to explore a spiritual love that was greater than my individual life and personal pain. I would suffer many trials before I was able to find direction. My understanding of the interior life and the holiness of creation were inchoate until one fateful October day in 1976.

It was on this day that God broke into my world, transforming my whole being and opening me to both the suffering and splendor of reality. I was felled to the ground by the intensity of suffering I witnessed. I was raised up by the transcendent inflow of divine love. While nothing since compares to the awe I experienced and the radical changes that took place within my heart and my soul, I share a recollection from my journals.

It was a beautiful, sunny day in Northern California. I walked into my friend's house from picking vegetables in the garden, feeling the warmth of the late morning sun streaming across the wooden floorboards. All at once, right in front of me the wall dividing the living room from the kitchen dissolved away, revealing an endless expanse of palpable light. The Light, more brilliant and denser than earthly light, advanced with such intensity that I fell to my knees and then to the ground, my legs no longer able to hold my weight. I lay down on my side on the warm floor and my body began to tremble. Looking up at the white curtains gently framing the window above my head, I remember thinking how harmonious, how wise, everything is.

As Light beyond Light pressed into me with greater force, I started to vibrate until my whole being was stretched to an edge of emotional endurance. Every sense was heightened. My body could barely hold the magnitude of awe, of being consumed by a higher order of passion and wisdom. If my mind were capable of forming a thought, I would have marveled at how immediate, how profound, how benevolent the universe was. I would have been able to describe the feeling of being enraptured by love, as if every atom, every cell within me were a hymn of praise.

But I had no words. Ceding myself to the soft wood and blazing light, tears filled my eyes.

Now an intense suffering racked my body. Acute pains were crushing my heart, choked, stabbing sobs in my throat. My wounded heart became everyone's wound, and the agony of this suffering broke open *The Suffering*. In wave after wave of anguish, suffering flowed into me. So intense was the pain that my heart broke open. I was shown the cause of suffering and the nature of suffering. Every suffering was my suffering: I was the stricken emaciated child in Ethiopia; the mother in El Salvador whose infant has no food; the Jews marched to gas chambers in Auschwitz and Treblinka; and the battered woman in Somalia. Every person who cried, every soldier killed in war, every tree sacrificed, every animal cruelty, every father who mourned and every woman violated was my suffering.

As the hours passed the suffering became more intense until my breath was its breath, and my heartbeat the measure of its pulse. Tossed in the whirlwind of human violence, intense pain pierced my heart and my throat, as the fire of suffering turned my illusions to ash. I was God suffering. The Holy One suffered; God suffered the suffering. The suffering annihilated me and left me vulnerable, spent. I died in the suffering. I died suffering. There was no me.

The pain of seeing the Suffering God, the Divine who suffers, was almost more than my heart could bear. The pain of experiencing that Holy Mystery suffers and we do nothing to alleviate suffering killed me. Forever stamped and wedded to Her plight, I had seen the wounded heart of the Divine.

Afternoon ceded to night. The suffering itself, its explosive power forever changing who and what I am, became the catalytic force of entrance into a new world. The whole room shimmered with lights. The air, thick with angelic figures and great, expansive wings, quivered with sound. Delicate layers of visible energy, pulsating and radiating in multiple colors surrounded each person and object. I was exquisitely tender, as if the boundary between every one of my limbs and the world had dissolved, allowing me to see with the eyes of my soul and hear with the ears of my spirit. The tree outside the window, the couch at the edge of my foot, and my own eye looking upon them were joined in an invisible communion.

Silence now descended upon me, its great gravitational pull causing the waves of pain to recede. Impressed into my soul and the cells of my body was a Presence so comprehensive and a Love so intense that they were concrete, more real than my friend sitting before me, more substantial than the giant redwood outside our door. I was pinned to the floor. The heavy, condensed weight of these divine energies turned its illuminative force upon me, restructuring the cells of my body and the memories of my soul. My awareness ascended until divine realms cradled in radiating folds of light surrounded me. At the distant reaches of my innermost sight, a regal figure stood guard before the portal of an infinite majesty I later name Most Holy and Unnamable Presence. Like the tide rushing back to the shore, from Her innermost depths came a torrent of love so total, so complete that my heart could barely contain its joy.

Perhaps I was now on a couch or still on the floor. But I sat up and it felt as though I was suspended on a raised platform. I turned up face upward, fully attentive with every fiber of my being to words without sound, to Wisdom pouring into the top of my head. More than vision or illumination, this was an inflow of divine truth, a comprehensiveness only to be grasped whole, indivisible. As if the collective storehouse of mystery were revealed all at once, implanted into my soul, and opened by love, the key that unlocked everything.

But despite the lack of mental tracking, I did *know* and *understand* in a depth of awareness beyond thought. As I write, I can still take myself back to that night as luminous records of wisdom and knowledge populated my consciousness, transfiguring my reality away from the past and into the future, nourishing my being not from the waters of Christianity or Judaism or any named tradition, but from the fountain of unplumbed truth.

And there and then I was a disciple of this new Way, and all that I would ever do and be in this life was established in my being.

Surrounded by beauty, I understood the purpose of life, which solely existed as a tribute to the Divine. I watched the world's sorrow and pain coalesce in a band of fog, a superficial covering over the splendor that lay beneath. Concealed was a unifying force raising everything up to its own incandescence. I swam in an ocean of surrender. There was neither past nor future. No error had been committed. We were all untouched by history or fate, washed clean of any misdeeds.

Annihilated, compelled by this radiant splendor too beautiful for words, all suffering was anointed and bathed in an immense joy. Stamped into whatever it is we name "I am" was a vast openness, a Heart concealed within a Heart, the fiery flame of another way. This was the site of our sin-less-ness; this was the Source from which all blessing flowed. In the luminescent darkness, silence defied and exceeded any truth yet spoken and knew with an unknowing every word uttered. As the watch of the night passed, a new Revealing took form. Impressed into me were ancient truths and future truths yet to be born. I knew by whom I am known and understood by the force of understanding itself.

Yet I cannot say that what was revealed was love or light or wisdom, or every word ever spoken or every thought in the mind of the world. Or even whether it was every hidden mystery, every sublime affirmation of love, or every tree of glory, because the beat of my heart, my life, was bound to its flow. Everything I needed to know was given. Everything I ever yearned for and prayed for was offered. This love, this generosity broke my heart.

Weak and fragile, I opened my eyes to find that the wheel of night had turned to dawn. I lifted myself up from the floor and looked around. In one fatal span, time and history were changed. Everywhere there was nothing but the Divine imprint. Brought to the brink of death, the sheer passion of the Holy had invaded my separateness and claimed me for its own.

While the comprehensiveness of the experience can never be fully imparted, I list five significant aftereffects that have stayed with me to this day.

- Human cruelty, suffering, and violence wound the Divine. God bears our suffering. My life must be on the side of mercy and justice. As planetary citizen and as mother, I committed myself to alleviating pain and to resisting the forces of violence and oppression.
- Religious divisions and claims of superior truth, culture, gender, race, or sexual orientation violate the universal principle of love. Whoever degrades the circle of belonging harms every being and wounds the divine heart. I committed myself to be a devotee of peace, to honor religious diversity, and to never privilege my truth or my religion over another.
- A new vision of the sacred came into the world—one that I associated with the Divine Mother, which I later named, *via feminina*. This revelatory landscape is spiritually nonviolent, ethically merciful, and theologically open. It heralds a new dimension of spiritual life, perhaps a new way of being human.
- All creation is one and universal. This insight of the mystical coinherence of all realities challenged me to fulfill its demands of an embodied worldview—a truly global, earth-based spirituality inclusive of all beings and open to the transcendent.
- This radical event was far more comprehensive than a vision or transient glimpse of the Holy. It was the inception of a spiritual path—a Way—of truth into the heart of reality. It was the road to total inner transformation that would require a vow of obedience to the monk within me.

Immediately after this series of revelations, I left behind the life I had known. Before long, I was offering classes on contemplation and serving as a spiritual companion to people within and outside religious affiliation. The common denominator in this period was my desire to grow closer to God and to help others embrace the contemplative call. For those who felt disenfranchised by their religion, or who were exploring a renewal of faith, I encouraged them to find God within. Before religion or identity is the mystical capacity intrinsic to personhood. It is the birth-right of everyone.

Mystical Dialogue

I returned to academia to pursue a doctorate in historical theology, writing my dissertation on Meister Eckhart's "Desert of the Godhead" or "*gotheit.*" In Eckhart's mysticism, the Desert of the Godhead was beyond the Christian Trinity of Father, Son, and Holy Spirit. Depicted in the Meister's sermons as "neither this nor that," the *gotheit* was the fount of transformation and the renewal of sacred consciousness in the soul.

In Eckhart's divine desert I recognized elements of my own experience. The Meister's dynamic description of the mutual interpenetration of the Trinity and the Godhead, where even God "becomes and unbecomes," pointed the way toward the intradivine basis for the dialogue of religions. Dialogue among and openness to all religions was built into deep structures of consciousness. Reality was dialogic. God was on the side of openness, freedom. My faith experience outside of religion, and faith experiences of others whom I had met or counseled, emerged from the divine nature itself.

Further, in Eckhart's claim that the detached soul breaks through (*durchbruch*) even the highest levels of a religion's metaphysics, I found a mystical foundation for the dialogue of religions. At the core of every religion is a meta-theology, a nothingness that is overarching of the various particular theologies and religious philosophies. It is also a deconstructive process that prepares the soul to receive the primacy of divine love. Although every religion extols love, an element of tribalism is attached to the claim. Eckhart exhorts the soul to shed self-importance, for detachment is higher than particular love. Detached love is love that ameliorates the suffering caused by false holiness and pride. It promotes an ethic of love for the world, which seeks the spiritual wellbeing of the whole. It explicitly guards against possessiveness and claims of superiority. It operates on the principle of nonviolence, looking for ways to persuade hearts and minds.

During graduate-school and after, while a faculty at Liberal Arts Colleges, I was privileged to participate in lively conferences with leading thinkers in the spiritual dialogue of religions, among them Raimon Panikkar, Ewert Cousins, Moshe Idel, Houston Smith, Bernard McGinn, and Krishna Sivaraman. From them I learned it was through the dialogue of religious experience, through sharing of one's faith and mystical apprehension of reality that one entered a point of ultimate depth. Often the most profound realizations took place during times of silence.

Sophia-Wisdom

While my October 1976 experience was implicitly a revelation of the Divine Feminine, it wasn't until I completed graduate studies that I realized its explicit call. Kneeling in front of a statue of the Madonna in the Minnesota woods, suddenly I was overcome with the realization that Sophia was the hidden voice beneath everything. For the first time I understood that her elusive wisdom had been guiding me all along. I decided to read everything I could: the Russian Sophiologists, Thomas Merton's devotion to Sophia in the figure of Proverb, and female and male mystics who experienced the power of the Divine Feminine.

Sophia freed me from the defense of the separate self. I accepted the path I had been following was an emerging contemplative tradition. Global in orientation, ecumenical and interspiritual in its depth, this was a complete mystical quest, leading the devotee to a God-experience alongside, but different from, known historical religions. It functioned outside of patriarchy. There was no need to reject any authentic faith or diminish ancient truths.

The way of the Divine Feminine is essential to the future of our planet. Sophia's wisdom is silence, because she precedes word and knowledge. Yet she speaks everywhere. She is inexhaustible nothingness, the emptiness of no form. She is the unseen in every presence. She cannot be owned or possessed. It is only through her that the soul returns to its source. The shining face of Mercy, she heals all our sins.

Via Feminina

While teaching a class on the early Christian mystics I coined the term *via feminina*. In describing two Christian paths of union with God—*via positiva and via negativa*—I found myself saying there was a third way— the way of the feminine, or the feminine way—*via feminina*. I was immediately struck by the power of the phrase because it evoked the classical spiritual paths and situated the feminine within the lineage of revelation and prophetic history. Within its historical context, the Latin word "*via*," meaning "road" or "way," signifies the spiritual journey we take toward union with God. Having chosen the word *via feminina*, I wanted to convey a quality of consciousness and a mystical path that includes, but is not confined, to categories of biological sex or attributes of gender construction. The way of the feminine is present in both women and men; nevertheless, I hold that feminine consciousness is embodied and expressed differently in females than in males.

Via feminina represents a spiritual path and process of inner transformation. As representative of a turn in the mystical path to God, it appropriates and goes beyond the function of the apophatic, or negative journey, as situated within its Western theological context. As a constructed phrase, *via feminina* is related to the spiritual quests and language structures of the classical traditions; but it also disturbs and transgresses them. Standing outside or beyond the logic that formed their language, spirituality, and theology, it mystically functions as a continual unsaying, a continual disruption of the previous thousands of years of saying from patriarchal cultures and religions. Rereading the classical archetype, *via feminina* extends the apophatic process not only to language and conceptual ideas about God, but also to the gender disparity codified within its spiritual practices and contemplative paths. It thus involves a radical type of ontological negation that pulls up the roots of misogyny and seeds of oppression that have been handed down from generation to generation and planted in our souls.

Yet *via feminina* is not only a path for women. It has efficacy for anyone who places primary importance on the recognition and elimination of all interlocking forms of oppression. Spiritual liberation today involves an awareness of the interrelationship between embodiment and transcendence that constitutes the whole person. It pays particular attention to integrate the multiple wisdoms of body, psyche, and soul in order to name and heal what offends, diminishes, or violates the person. Its single most distinguishing feature is that as a spiritual path it does not transcend differences—whether of gender, culture, race, or sex—but enters into them to forge a deeper unity in one's soul and to heal the underlying causes of suffering. Thus, *via feminina* is vigilant to the ways in which the categories that name and define the spiritual life (redemption, salvation, soul, self, God, virtue) as well as the processes or stages of mystical ascent (purgation, dark night, union) repeat subtle forms of gender, racial, sexual, or social violence.

The fact that the spiritual journey has been dominated over the centuries by patriarchal thinking, unjust relations, and oppression of women and other outsiders indicates that there is a dimension of the soul that is not free, a place where, as a world community, we are not yet committed to actualizing the dignity of all beings and the promise of liberation or salvation.

New Landscapes of the Sacred

Global contemplative consciousness and the way of the feminine are intertwined in my work. They reveal previously unseen vistas and distant horizons. They offer hope that a different manner of being—a more holy and sensitive way of doing things—is breaking into consciousness.

- These new landscapes of the sacred are premised on the unconditional love radiating from the merciful heart of Reality. If a religion is exclusive, violent, oppressive, or dismissive of the equality of all beings, then it is not a complete spirituality. This is foundational to the divine quest. All must be included in the circle of belonging. None left out of the banquet of love.

- These new landscapes of the sacred encourage new sacred expressions, recognizing that there is not one final and only revelation. They foster participation in new faith traditions and are committed to healing old patterns of religious and spiritual thought that promote segregation and violence.

- These new landscapes of the sacred offer a spiritual path for the whole of creation, not only for humans, not only for women. These are spiritual ways of being that take into account the panoply of beings, the cosmic circle, and our more-than-human kin. They thus require an ethic of *amor mundi*, love of the world.

- These new landscapes of the sacred uphold a consciousness of vulnerability, receptivity, and tenderness. They recognize that global contemplative consciousness draws the soul into deeper intimacy with the divine nature, both in suffering and in joy. It thus requires a new understanding of the spiritual life, of the depth to which the soul identifies with and carries the burden of divine compassion.

- These new landscapes of the sacred are embedded in the world. The mystical force reaches down into our hearts and emerges up from the earth to protect the dignity of all beings, including the social realities, politics, and religions that serve humanity. The spiritual journey is neither gender neutral nor free from the social impediments of its historical development. The true mystic must be concerned for the whole of creation and work toward its sanctification.

- These new landscapes of the sacred reveal new understandings of the Divine, however named, and are contemporary expressions of Spirit on Earth.

Taking a Stand

In 1993 I became an ordained interfaith chaplain. That same year I formed the nonprofit Desert Interfaith Church, followed in 1997 by the formation of the Interfaith Theological Seminary. Both initiatives were motived by a belief that the entire human community is the inheritor of the world's sacred traditions; no one should be excluded from sacramental rites or spiritual practices because he or she has not vowed allegiance to church, mosque, synagogue, or the like; and when people of different religious and nonreligious backgrounds join together for prayer and contemplative reflection, a global sign of peace forms.

Holding weekly services at a variety of locations, including private homes and university chapels, our prayer service involved reading spiritual texts and scriptures from the world's religions. Focused on a weekly contemplative theme, the time together was spent in silence, contemplative reflection, and sharing a sacred rite.

The Interfaith Theological Seminary was founded to educate and ordain women and men in interfaith ministry. Committed to spiritual equality of gender and of sacramental roles, the Seminary's mission was to minister to all people, promoting peace and healing. Our educational program was two years long and was focused on the contemplative heart of reality. Coursework covered eight areas: monastic and mystical studies, the philosophy and practice of interfaith, the world's religions and sacred texts, spiritual direction, spirituality of nonviolence, new religious paradigms, pastoral theology and ministry, and healing and spirituality. Students were required to complete a social-justice and pastoral-arts internship. The Seminary also affiliated with Prescott College, affording students a joint MA and Seminary degree. Lacking funding sources or other endowments, these programs are no longer active.

Returning to Monastic Roots

In all of these life changes, the underlying call to solitude and silence never left me. But it was not until I was on a sabbatical that I formally professed monastic vows. The process was assisted and witnessed by a small community of women Benedictine monks. Drawing on the universal call to monasticism, my vows were not made under the auspices of Benedictines or Christianity. Neither were they a rejection of these ancient traditions. Rather, I took vows of commitment to the monastic heart of reality, to that enduring center that precedes religious identification and institutional form. I took vows to love God with everything I am and to serve others through love.

Taking profession was a transformative spiritual experience. The ceremony itself was simple and beautiful. My consciousness was further re-formed around silence, simplicity, and solitude. Practically, I now assessed everything in my environment from this perspective: what brings me closer to Holy Mystery, what offers peace, great silence? I am certain that the monastic call is intrinsic to all people and is not confined to religious organizations or orders. It is a free call within the self, one that is born with us into the world and to which we owe allegiance. The years I spent avoiding the monk within, too busy with family and work, and perhaps afraid that it would make me more different or too pious, were empty concerns. Because there is nothing more natural than to affirm one's monastic nature, living in God's time, seeking transformation into the heart of reality, and loving creation with one's whole soul.

The monastic archetype will take new forms during this century and those to come. The Great Vocation will evolve, as the human heart grows closer to the divine heart.

Schola Divina and the Community of a New Monastic Way

I am indebted to the world's religions and sacred wisdoms. They have been beacons of light and solace for my soul. Yet, I also have experienced bias, disbelief, disdain, and outright cruelty against myself and other women by the guardians of a particular worldview or orthodoxy. As a spiritual director, I have listened to painful stories of religious sisters, women clergy, and spiritual women who have been ridiculed, excoriated, and defamed by the power elites within their faith tradition. Women must rise up and claim their inherent right to speak of Truth, to speak for God, and to demand the world community foster compassion and love for all the Earth's creatures and children. More than ever, I realize that the liberation of women's spirits and the prophetic voice of women are essential to the survival of our planet.

Within the context of my life experience, I formed Schola Divina (Latin, "divine school") as the teaching arm of my work. The name "divine school" signifies that all wisdom comes from God. Under the auspices of Schola Divina, I have offered numerous workshops and retreats on global contemplative spirituality, on new conversations in spiritual direction, on the monk within, and on insight into the path of living for Truth and in Holy Wisdom. I also developed a two-year program of monastic studies, which culminates in participants taking monastic vows.

Students from my earliest days of teaching have been together for more than forty years. Together we have formed a remarkable, stable community, the Community of a New Monastic Way. We have remained faithful to the original revelation received in 1976 and continue to explore its many and varied expressions. We have practiced an authentic spiritual path, one open to all religions but centered in the mystical and feminine heart of reality. Despite our members' living around the country, we stay in contact throughout the year via phone and the Internet. We also come together as a group usually twice a year for an extended week of study, prayer, and reflection. We envision our work as one of forging a global monastic path, one that honors the contemplative heart of reality and the mercy of nonviolence. Love is always the measure of truth. We frequently discuss the meaning of belonging without boundaries, being committed to our path without being exclusive or superior, and welcoming others to share with us. But more than this, we are bond by our love of the Divine, by seeking total interior transformation to the best of our abilities and in the context of our contemporary lives. In this way we aspire to be true monks, mystical monks open to the world.

* * *

Questions for Discussion

1. Beverly listed "five significant aftereffects" of her profound mystical experience. Consider the relevance and implications of these aftereffects given your own context. What do you think would change if you began to incorporate them into your life and the life of your community?

2. Beverly spoke of undergoing "a deconstructive process that prepares the soul to receive the primacy of divine love." To what extend have you undergone—or need to undergo—a "deconstructive process" in your own spiritual journey? What do you think requires deconstruction and how might *reconstruction* take place? What insights does Beverly offer?

3. What is the significance of the *via feminina* for yourself and your community? How does Beverly distinguish this "way" from the *via positiva* and *via negativa*?

4. Revisit the "new landscapes of the sacred" as Beverly expresses them. Which are most impactful for you and your community? How might these collectively alter the spiritual geography of our time?

5. Beverly admitted to spending years "avoiding the monk within."

In what ways have you done the same? What concrete steps can you take to awaken your own monastic nature?

Sages to Explore

- Meister Eckhart
- Raimon Panikkar
- Ewert Cousins
- Moshe Idel
- Houston Smith

- Bernard McGinn
- Krishna Sivaraman
- Thomas Merton
- The Russian Sophiologists

2: *The Journey of a Devout Skeptic*

Peter Russell

I never imagined spirituality would be so important in my life. I was brought up Anglican, in a loose sort of way. We went to church once a month or so, as did others in the village—a sort of keeping in good favor with God. At age thirteen, I went through the process of confirmation, during which I was told that the Nicene Creed was the core belief—that is, *the creed* of Christianity, and something I was meant to sign off on. I'd thought it was just another one of those things one chanted in church: "I believe in one God, the father almighty, maker of Heaven and Earth... and in Jesus Christ, his only Son... born of the virgin Mary..." etc. I realized I couldn't possibly believe in this. I told my parents so, and that I didn't want to go church anymore. They were understanding and accepting, and I never did go to church again. Many years later my mother confided in me that she never really believed it herself. And I suspect many others in the congregation didn't either.

Throughout childhood and my student years I always thought I would become a scientist. I loved discovering how the world worked. Why is the sky blue? What makes the wind blow? Why does iron rust? How do plants know when to bloom? How do planes fly? Why are snowflakes six-pointed stars?

The more I discovered, the more fascinated I became. At sixteen I was devouring Einstein and marveling at the paradoxical world of quantum physics. I delved into theories of how the universe began, and pondered the mysteries of space and time. I had a passion for knowing, an insatiable curiosity, and a need to understand the laws and principles that governed the world.

I was not, however, a materialist, believing that everything could be explained by the physical sciences. I had a growing interest in the untapped potentials of the human mind. Stories of yogis buried alive for days or lying on beds of nails, intrigued me. I dabbled in so-called out-of-body experiences and experimented with the altered states of consciousness produced by hyperventilating or pulsating lights. I also developed my own technique of meditation, although, at the time, I did not recognize it as such.

Nevertheless, my overriding interest was still in the physical sciences, and above all, mathematics. So when the time came to select a subject to study at university, the choice was obvious. And so was the choice of university. Cambridge was the best British university for studying mathematics.

The Turning Point

In my third year at Cambridge, I was exactly where I thought I wanted to be, studying in the best of universities, surrounded by truly inspiring minds. I even had Stephen Hawking as a tutor for a while. Yet something else was stirring inside me. I could solve Shrödinger's wave equation for hydrogen, a remarkable success of theoretical physics that not only describes the structure of hydrogen but predicts some of its properties. The most fascinating question for me was: How had hydrogen—the first and most basic element in the universe—evolved into a system that could know about hydrogen, and do the mathematics that described it? How had the universe become self-conscious?

It was becoming clear that however much science I studied it would not address this more fundamental question—let alone answer it. I found myself reading more about mind and consciousness, and focusing less on my mathematical assignments. After much heart-searching, I decided to change course and study experimental psychology; it seemed the closest academic approach to understanding consciousness.

Yet, despite all I learned about neurophysiology, biochemistry, memory, behavior, and perception, I found myself no closer to understanding the nature of consciousness itself. Indeed, I do not recall the word "consciousness" having ever been mentioned during the course.

Eastern traditions seemed to have a lot to say about consciousness, and so had many mystics from around the world. For thousands of years, they had focused on the realm of the mind, exploring its subtleties through direct personal experience. This, I realized, was the way to study consciousness, not by attaching electrodes to the scalp, but by a direct exploration of one's own consciousness. I began delving into ancient texts such as The Upanishads, The Tibetan Book of the Great Liberation, The Cloud of Unknowing, and works of contemporary writers such as Alan Watts, Aldous Huxley, Carl Jung, and Christopher Isherwood. At the same time, I began to investigate different forms of meditation.

Opening to Spirituality

First, I explored Buddhist practices, but wasn't that enthralled by the results. It seemed a lot of discipline was required, and I didn't have much of that. Then I came across Transcendental Meditation (TM). It was the summer of 1967 and The Beatles had just met the Maharishi, and with great enthusiasm. So, when a few months later his book, *The Science of Being and Art of Living*, caught my eye in a library I decided to look into it.

Everything he was saying about meditation was the exact opposite of everything I'd been reading, or had been taught. Yet it made much more sense. Whereas other teachings I had come across were talking about effort and mental discipline, he was advocating complete effortlessness in meditation. Effort he claimed just made the mind more tense, which was the opposite to the mind of becoming more relaxed. He was turning everything inside out in a way that made sense to me.

I decided I must try his form of meditation. And it worked—from the very first day. I found it easy to settle into a quieter state of mind; moreover, it was enjoyable. My TM teacher soon became a mentor. Over the next six months, I spent a lot of time listening to his talks, reading his writings, or just chatting with him. What he gave me, which I needed so much, was an intellectual satisfaction. He quenched my thirst for a deeper understanding of meditation—how it worked and where it could lead.

The following summer Maharishi was leading a retreat in Italy. I made my way there in order to sit at the feet of the master. The days were a mix of meditations and talks he gave to the hundred or so of us assembled. We also had private interviews with him. During one, he invited me to go to India the next spring, along with The Beatles and other celebrities, on what later became a somewhat infamous course. I was, needless to say, very keen on going. But it would have been in the final months of my undergraduate course, and I knew I needed to get that degree; so I reluctantly declined. Had I gone, I would no doubt have many stories of that trip with which to regale people.

A year later, after completing my degree, the opportunity re-presented itself. Without hesitation I went, driving out from England to India—quite a story in itself. The course that I was on took a very different direction from the one with The Beatles. Many of the participants were young people like myself, keen to learn, along with people conducting scientific research on TM. We grilled the Maharishi on just about every aspect of his teaching, going deep into Indian philosophy, and his own *Advaita* tradition—what today is known as nonduality. What I learned there became a major influence on my thinking and has informed much of my teaching and writing over the years.

My time in India was a second turning point in my life. I realized that there might, after all, be something to the various religions—or rather to the spiritual teachings that gave rise to them. I saw that, in one way or another, they were showing how we get caught in limited ways of seeing the world, self-centered attitudes, attachments to material things, or a false sense of identity—all of which lead to suffering rather than happiness. Each tradition offered practices designed to liberate people from their suffering, and to discover their true nature. This is not to say that I came to accept the conventional religion I had rejected as a teenager, but I could see where it had come from. And this began to fascinate me.

I also came to see how so many of the problems we face in the world—personal, social, and global—stem from human decisions, which in turn are influenced by self-centered ways of thinking that the various traditions urged us to awaken from. It became clear that the spiritual awaking of humanity is an urgent need. Along with everything else we might do to solve the various problems facing us, we also need to tend to their roots. Otherwise, we are just fire-fighting one symptom of the underlying malaise after another. It became my personal mission to distil the common core of the world's various spiritual traditions, and present it in language appropriate to contemporary times.

On my return, I established a meditation center in Cambridge, and began doctoral research on the psychology of meditation, out of which came my first book, *The TM Technique: A Skeptics Guide*. I started to explore more deeply the relationship of brain and mind, and the fascinating question of the nature of reality.

What Is Real?

One thing became clear from my studies of the brain: we do not see reality as it is, only a reconstruction of it.

Take vision, for example. When I see a tree, light from the tree forms an image on the retina of my eye. Photo-sensitive cells in the retina discharge electrons, triggering electro-chemical impulses that travel down the optic nerve to the visual cortex of the brain. There the data undergoes a complex processing that detects shapes, patterns, colors, and movements. The brain then integrates this information into a coherent whole, creating its picture of what it concludes is "out there." Finally, an image of the tree appears in my consciousness.

The same is true of every other quality we experience. Pressure waves in the air are experienced as sounds, chemical molecules stimulating the tongue or nose become tastes or smells, changes in the skin are experienced as touch and other sensations. In every case we seem to be experiencing the external world directly, but in truth all that we experience is a representation of the world appearing in our consciousness.

Around this time, I came cross the nineteenth-century German philosopher Immanuel Kant, who had come to similar conclusions without the benefit of neuroscience. He argued that all we ever know are the *phenomena* arising in our experience. The "thing-in-itself," what he called the *noumenon*, we never know directly. This doesn't mean we don't know anything about it. But all our knowledge of the world comes from exploring the representation of it in the mind, and from that drawing conclusions about the world "out there." Science aims to do just this— to deduce how the physical world operates. But all we discover—all we know and understand about the world, all our scientific theories and mathematical equations, our concepts of matter, energy, space, and time, our ideas about quarks, strings, particles, and waves—are but phenomena in the mind. We never have a direct knowing of the world.

The Divine Within

Kant went further and argued that not only is the thing-in-itself, *the transcendental object of experience*, unknowable, so is *the transcendental subject of all experience*, the "I" that is aware of the phenomena arising in the mind. This tied in with the Maharishi's teachings, the purpose of TM being to transcend all thought and come to rest in the stillness of the transcendental, or pure Self.

The same idea was coming up again and again in my readings of the mystics. Moreover, they were describing their awakening to this essential aspect of their being as a deep inner union with the divine. Some have expressed this blatantly in the statement "I am God." To many, this sounds blasphemous. God is not a human being, but the supreme deity, the almighty, eternal creator. How can any lowly human being claim that he or she is God? When the fourteenth-century Christian priest and mystic Meister Eckhart preached that "God and I are One," he was brought before Pope John XXII and forced to "recant everything that he had falsely taught." Not all were so lucky. The tenth-century Islamic mystic al-Hallāj was crucified for using language that claimed an identity with God.

To those who do not believe in God, such statements are not blasphemous so much as the symptoms of some delusion or pathology. In the modern scientific era, God seems a totally unnecessary concept. Science has looked into deep space, across the breadth of creation to the edges of the universe. It has looked back in "deep time" to the beginning of the universe. And it has looked down into the "deep structure" of the cosmos, to the fundamental constituents of matter. From quarks to quasars, it finds no evidence of God. Nor does it find any need for God. The universe seems to work perfectly well without any divine assistance. Thus, anyone talking of a personal identity with God is clearly talking nonsense.

But the one realm science has yet to explore is that of "deep mind." Those who *have* investigated this realm are the mystics, yogis, rishis, roshis, lamas, shamans, and other spiritual adepts who have explored consciousness firsthand. They have delved beneath the surface levels of the mind, observed the arising and passing of thought, and looked beyond that to the essence of their consciousness, to that ever-present and unchanging sense of "I," the transcendental subject of all experience. Time and again they have referred to this in spiritual terms. Ramana Maharshi probably put it best when he said, echoing the Torah, "*I am* is the name of God." They go on to describe this experience in terms of peace, love, truth, compassion, omnipresence, eternal—all qualities associated with more traditional ideas of God. This alternative, more mystical notion of God made far more sense to me than the one I had been brought up with. Moreover, it made God something to be experienced rather than believed in.

The Thought System of God

This realization gained a more practical value when, a few years later, I came across the book, *A Course in Miracles*. The miracles it refers to are not some miraculous events in the world, but the miracle of a shift in perception, in particular the shift from the thought system of the ego to the thought system of God.

Many find it a challenging book, partly because of its Christian language and use of the male pronoun, and because it is a long and heavy text, accompanied by 365 lessons. In addition, people often take its words literally, which can easily lead to confusion or dogmatism—particularly in terms of the word "God." I found that by interpreting "God" as the light of consciousness shining in us all—that is, the transcendental self—the course proved not only very insightful, and another reflection of nonduality, but also valuable in my own journey.

We tend to think of ego as some part of me, some other form of self. But when I observe my own experience, I may find various thoughts about what I want, what would make me happy, or give me more control over my world—what we might label "egocentric" thoughts. But I don't find a distinct self, or ego—an entity that is having these thoughts. What I call ego is not some "part" of me; it is a mode of thinking that is concerned with my well-being and survival. At times this thought system can be valuable. If there is some physical need to be taken care of, or some danger that needs to be avoided, then it is an important mode of thinking. But for most of us today, we get caught in this way of thinking when there is no physical need or danger. The net effect of this egoic thinking is to veil the inner peace and love that are intrinsic to the true Self. Hence the stated goal of the course: to remove the blocks to awareness of love's presence.

How to do this? The key learning for me was its suggestion to inquire if there were another way of seeing things; to ask for a different perspective from the ego's thought system. This I developed into a powerful, and most beneficial, form of prayer.

We usually think of prayer as an appeal to some higher power. We might pray for someone's healing, for success in some venture, for a better life, or for guidance on some challenging issue. Behind such prayers is the belief that we don't have the power to change things ourselves—if we did, we'd simply get on with the task. So, we beseech a higher power to intervene on our behalf.

But what really needs changing? Usually, we want the world to change. We want the circumstances we think will make us happy—or conversely, avoid those that will make us suffer. However, when we look more closely at why we aren't happy, we may find that the root lies not so much in the situation at hand, but in how we perceive it. In which case, it makes more sense to ask, not for an intervention in the world, but for an intervention in our minds. For that's where help is needed most.

So that is what I pray for. I settle into a quiet state, then ask with an attitude of innocent curiosity: "Could there, perhaps, be another way of seeing this?" I don't try to answer the question myself; to do so would doubtless activate my ego-mind, which loves to try to work out what to do. So, I simply pose the question. Let it go. And wait. Often a new way of seeing then dawns on me. It doesn't come as an idea, but as an actual shift in perception. I find myself seeing the situation in a new way, free from the ego's thought system.

The results of praying like this never cease to impress me. I find my fears and grievances dropping away. In their place is a sense of ease. Whoever or whatever was troubling me, I now see through more loving and compassionate eyes. Moreover, in this practice, I am not praying to some external power. I am praying to my Self, the divine essence in me, for guidance; to the unperturbed mind that sees things as they are without the overlay of the ego-mind's hopes and fears. The net result is that I found a way to allow "God" into my life. And to guide me on my journey.

An Atheist Who Believes in the Divine

As I've continued to explore into the depth of my being, my experience has both deepened and clarified. And the more I delve, the more I appreciate what the great masters have spoken of. Through all of this, my earlier scientific training has led me to maintain a healthy skepticism in these matters. For me, it is important not to take anything on faith, or because some wise or famous person has said it, or many people believe it. Only when something matches my own experience do I take it on board.

Today when people ask me if I believe in God, I usually say no. They are most likely referring to some monotheistic notion of God. In that sense I remain an atheist—that is, a non-theist. I do not believe in a creator of the universe, intervening in it and sustaining a personal relation to it creatures.

On the other hand, as should be clear, I do believe there is a universal experience of oneness, peace, love, freedom that many people have been blessed with. It may have come through dedicated spiritual practice, deep devotion, facing a hard challenge, or sometimes simply unbidden, out of the blue—a timeless moment in which one's personal dramas paled in the light of a deep inner peace and serenity. However it came, it usually led to a delightful joy in being alive, an unconditional love for all beings, and the dissolution of a personal self.

If one were living in a Judeo-Christian culture, it would be natural to interpret that as some connection with God. In the Hindu world, with a blessing from Krishna or some other deity. In a Buddhist culture, as an opening to one of the immeasurable states of mind. Or, in the less religious culture that many of us live in today, as simply awakening to our true Self.

* * *

Questions for Discussion

1. In his youth, Peter realized that he couldn't "possibly *believe*" the statements of the Nicene Creed. Instead, he sought living experience. What is the relationship between "belief" and "experience" in your own life? When they conflict do you tend to hold onto your belief or do you trust your experience and let your beliefs evolve?

2. Peter experienced the difference between *effort* and *effortlessness* in his spiritual practice and it made all the difference. Are you expending unnecessary effort when there should be effortlessness in your own spiritual path? Can you give some examples of where this might be the case?

3. Peter's mystical explorations revealed God to be "something to be experienced rather than believed in." What do you think he means by this? In what ways might this apply to your own spiritual journey?

4. In what ways might you also be an "atheist who believes in the divine"? Do the images of God you clearly reject make way for an image of God you can actually accept? What is the positive value of atheism for the spiritual journey?

5. Peter developed a method of prayer that was unique and transformative. What might change if you began to approach prayer in the form of *questions* rather than *requests*? What if prayer is more about *listening* and less about *speaking*? What then?

Sages to Explore

- Stephan Hawking
- Alan Watts
- Aldous Huxley
- Carl Jung
- Christopher Isherwood
- Ramana Maharshi
- Immanuel Kant

3: My Journey in Quest for the Purpose of Life
Ervin Laszlo

To recount the journey of my life is to tell the story of a quest to which I am deeply committed. It is a simple quest in conception, but challenging in practice. It is to find the purpose that underlies my life. I can say "my" life without being egocentric and blind to others, because I am convinced that the purpose that underlies my life is the purpose that underlies all life on the planet. To live up to this purpose is what endows my life with meaning.

I consider myself a rational person: I believe that genuine understanding is won by the logical linking of unambiguously defined terms and concepts. If the understanding concerns the real world, the terms and concepts need to be related to some form of perception of that world. However, finding the purpose of my life goes beyond the scope of empirical rationality. What I seek to understand does not follow from the concepts and relations I use to achieve that understanding. In the final count, finding the purpose of life—my life and all life—is a spiritual undertaking. I am committed to it and engaged in it. Thus, I could be called a spiritual person.

What does it take to be called *spiritual*? Some think that being spiritual means having either extra-ordinary, rationally-empirically inexplicable experiences, or having inborn or inbred convictions that go beyond the scope of the perceived world. I am not aware of having truly extraordinary experiences, except in regard to the purpose I believe underlies my life. I have a firm conviction that my life has purpose: it is not a series of events without rhyme or logic. There is purpose for my life, the same as for the life of everyone. This I believe intuitively, but I have real-world experiences that back it up. They testify that my intuitive belief is not just imagination.

I shall now recount the diverse stages of my adventurous lifelong journey in search of the purpose I believe underlies my life. But first I wish to acknowledge the role played in this journey by Caxrita Marjorie, the historic family Swedish-Finnish girl I married over sixty years ago. She has accompanied me through all the stages and phases of my life, providing a real home and being a warm and loving wife to me and mother to our sons. Without her, my journey could not have been undertaken, and certainly not have been taken to any meaningful level of satisfaction.

The Journey

My journey has unfolded in three distinct existences that roll into one. They took place in different places, with different people, under different circumstances. In retrospect, they appear to have been more than stages or phases of a single lifetime: they were whole reincarnations. Yet they had a common motif—a thread that runs through them and provides an element of consistency beyond all differences.

Concert pianist
The first stage was that of an internationally-acclaimed concert pianist. At the age of six or seven, it was discovered that I had an unusual talent for playing the piano. I played in a way that was natural to me, and apparently meaningful to others. Playing music on the piano meant a great deal to me. It meant entering an experience of wholeness and completeness, of spontaneously created and always re-created perfection. The

experience came of its own; I didn't seek it. It was the experience of a dynamic unfolding in a realm of beauty.

When I began to reflect on this experience, I shared it with my mother, who was my teacher and mentor. She said that it was the fruit of the work of great composers such as Wagner and Beethoven, producing works in the fullness of their genius. But I found that my experience came about most spontaneously in the music of romantic composers, such as Chopin and Brahms. It was most clearly catalyzed by works of playful genius, in music of unspeakable lightness and wholeness. There was also music of intrinsic perfection—every note being exactly as it had to be, unmodifiable and irreplaceable—that was my experience of Bach, Mozart, and Schubert.

I have always been happy to share my musical experience with others. I played concerts in public from the age of nine, sometimes as a soloist with symphony orchestras. Having a public audience heightened the experience, but playing it for myself alone gave more freedom. In my late teens and twenties, I began to appreciate and value this freedom. It was the freedom of trying not to do anything "for" or "to" anybody—just having the experience for its own sake. Then the mind could wander freely. Once I learned a piece of music, I did not need to think about performing it; my hands, indeed my entire body, played the notes and allowed me the freedom to feel and think whatever came to me. It was not a question of wanting to have or achieve anything, but of letting everything come on its own, giving it free rein. When I could enter the music and forget everything else, what came was a sense of wholeness, completeness, and perfection.

Unlike most concert artists, I was not content with just having this experience: I wanted to know what it was. What is its meaning, and what are its implications for me and my life?

Searching for answers called for moving beyond aesthetic enjoyment to intellectual inquiry. From my mid-twenties, when I started married life and life as a family man with a child, I found myself shifting from the keyboard of the piano to the keyboard of the typewriter. I had a small but trustworthy Remington portable on a desk across from my piano (it was just a step away—my classic Bechstein concert grand took up most of the room). When my free associations produced something that remained in my mind as meaningful and perhaps important, I got up from the piano and moved to the desk and I started typing.

I did not analyze what I was writing—I just allowed it to tumble onto the page. After all, I did not have to be critical of what appeared—I was not writing for anything or anybody else. I was only writing to satisfy myself. This was a kind of automatic writing—not entirely automatic, but clearly not under conscious control. I allowed my fingers to move over the keyboard. Being the fingers of a pianist, they moved fast. Almost as fast as the unfolding of the ideas that appeared in my mind. I filled page after page, and seldom read back what I had written.

Then the realization dawned on me that there must be others who have similar experiences, whether they were triggered by performing music or by something else. After all, there are entire libraries filled with research on aesthetic experiences. I would do well to consult this potential treasure-house.

There was also another motivation. I was reluctant to share what I wrote because it was mostly taken as the understandable hobby of a musician, to fill his spare time. And when someone took my ideas seriously—which happened time and again—I could not explain how I came by them. Scholarly people could not accept that I came up with them myself. Having written these notes without prior research seemed naïve and amateurish. Serious writing on philosophical topics is based on mountains of citations and references.

This concern ceased when my notes caught the eye of a publisher who read them and offered to publish them. This was in The Hague in Holland, where after a successful piano recital I was in an expansive mood and sat with a sympathetic listener to talk about my ideas. He asked if I ever wrote down what I was talking about, and when I said yes, I made notes but just for myself, he still wanted to see them. I always had my notes with me, and went to my hotel room to get them. The gentleman started to read and asked if he could borrow them for the night to read carefully—he would bring them back the next morning. I agreed, and the next morning he showed up with my notes and said that he would like to publish them. It would take some work to get them into shape as a publishable book, but he would help. He introduced himself: his name was Priem, and he was the philosophy editor of the noted Dutch philosophy and theology publisher Martinus Nijhoff. Thus, a year later in 1963, my first book, *Essential Society: An Ontological Reconstruction*, was born.

Based on this experience, I realized that my writing could have an interest for people, and henceforth sought to turn my ideas into documented ones. I looked for books I could learn from and also cite as references. I lived in Switzerland at the time, and had no difficulty finding bookstores offering a wide variety of books on science and philosophy. I began to browse and came across a heavily marked and annotated volume that appeared to be by an Indian philosopher, B.K. Mallik. It was published in Oxford in 1952, and was titled *Related Multiplicity*. It argued that everything in the world is an intrinsically connected multiplicity. This sounded relevant, and I began to read.

This was the first philosophy book I ever studied. It made a lasting impression on me. There was a reference to the work of philosopher Alfred North Whitehead that seemed particularly promising. I went back to the bookstore and ordered Whitehead's major work, *Process and Reality*. This was not an easy book to comprehend, but I read it avidly, over and over again.

Whitehead's philosophy changed not just how I thought about the world, but how I lived in it. The world around me changed from an ensemble of lifeless physical objects and chance-produced biological organisms to an organic network of interconnected wholes: embracing "societies" of "actual entities." The universe became a complete and perfect interconnected and interacting, indeed, inter-constituted whole. Things in it are what they are due to their connection to each other. Relations, not substances, are of the essence. All things are nodal points in a cosmic network. The network as a whole has meaning; all other things derive their meaning by being a part of it.

I began to see the world in this new and strange, but soon familiar light. Nothing in the world merely *is*—everything tends, grows, develops. It develops into, and develops as, an interconnected whole. This is evolution. It is not evolution in the classical biological sense where it refers to changes in the gene pool of living species; it is evolution in the cosmic, universal sense—in how it refers to the constant and consistent transformation of everything with and by everything else.

One day I was traveling by train along the river Rhine. I was headed to Beethoven's native city, Bonn, where I was scheduled to give a concert with four of his major sonatas. This was a privilege, and I should have been fully taken up preparing for it. But I was not: I was in a different world. I saw the Rhine and saw that it was not a river but a "flowing." I saw the trees along the shores and they were not trees but "treeings." The clouds floating in the sky were "clouding." I found myself in a living, dynamic reality—a shattering, life-transforming experience.

I nearly forgot to get off the train at the Bonn station, and when I did, I reached my hotel in a daze. At the concert the next evening I had a shock. When I came to my senses, I found myself on stage in front of a distinguished audience. I realized that I was playing the second movement of Beethoven's Sonata opus 53, the "Waldstein Sonata," but didn't know whether I was playing the principal theme of that movement for the first or for the second time (that theme recurs at the end of the movement and then leads over to the third movement). If I guessed wrong, I would either repeat the entire second movement, or leave it out altogether. What a dilemma...a decision had to be made instantly. I chose to move to the third movement. It must have been the right choice, because nobody got up or started laughing or whistling.

Later that evening I said to myself, this is not good and it cannot continue. I can't serve two masters at the same time; I must follow my quest. I decided to leave a flowering career in music to devote myself to reading, reflection, and writing.

The opportunity to pursue my quest in a fertile environment was soon given. A few days prior to the incident in Bonn, I received an invitation from John Schrader, head of the philosophy department at Yale. He invited me to spend a semester at the university as a fellow. He knew that I had no formal qualifications for joining a department of philosophy (the sheepskin I had on my wall was the artist diploma of the Liszt Academy of Music in Budapest, hardly a qualification for joining a distinguished philosophy department). Schrader said this did not matter— he had read my recently published books (*Essential Society*, and the book that followed it in 1966, *Beyond Scepticism and Realism*) and wanted to have me cross-fertilize with similarly-minded philosophers. I decided to accept his invitation and went to New Haven, leaving behind—if only for a few months—my wife and child in Europe. As it turned out, I left behind a career as a concert artist.

Then the second stage of my journey began.

The academic philosopher

The environment for pursuing my interests at Yale was extraordinarily good. I met and made lasting friends with such illustrious scientist-philosophers as Henry Margenau and F.S.C. Northrop. I had access to any course offered at Yale, auditing any lecture I wished. I took full advantage of this opportunity. A host of ideas were buzzing in my head, waiting to be committed to paper.

I started drafting a highly researched book titled *Introduction to Systems Philosophy*. I owed the term "system" to Ludwig von Bertalanffy, the founder of General Systems Theory. Bertalanffy was not permanently at Yale, but he occasionally visited there. On one of these occasions, we met and established a professional connection that matured into deep friendship. He read the draft of my book on Systems Philosophy and wrote the foreword to it.

I received invitations from various academic sources and ended up as a professor of philosophy at the State University of New York's College at Geneseo. (By this time my formal academic qualifications had been assured: I was awarded the *Doctorat es-Lettres et Sciences Humaines*, the highest degree of the Sorbonne, the University of Paris, in 1970.) At Geneseo, I was given much freedom to pursue my ideas. I did so, greatly benefiting from contact with fellow-faculty members and my seminar students.

I would have been happy to pursue my quest for understanding the purpose of life through research, teaching, and writing at Geneseo, but an unexpected comment shook me up and impelled me further. Shortly after the publication of *Systems Philosophy*, the wife of a colleague remarked at a faculty party, "When are you going to write something that people can understand?" That struck a sensitive chord—can people really not understand the concept of universal connection between evolving systems? I must write in a way, I said to myself, that this basic idea becomes comprehensible to everybody. I went home and sat down to the typewriter (this was 1972, before home computers). Here is what the world truly is, I wrote: It is a world of evolving systems at all scales of size and complexity, from single-celled organisms to galaxies. They interact and evolve, creating more and more evolved and organized, coherent natural systems.

It was less than a week later when I sent a slim manuscript to my publisher titled *The Systems View of the World*. It was published in the same year as *Introduction to Systems Philosophy*. The latter took five years of thinking, writing, and rewriting, and this book took five days. It reached a sizable readership and catalyzed much discussion. It proved to be the tail that wagged the dog.

The renown realized by my writing and lecturing on systems thinking led to the next stage of my journey.

The humanist-activist

This stage first appeared in the form of a request from Richard Falk, director of the Center of International Studies at Princeton University.

He invited me to give a series of lectures at the principal lecture hall of the Woodrow Wilson School. The topic was to be the international system. I protested: I know very little about the international system and don't see what I could contribute. He said never mind: he and his colleagues will provide the interpretation—what they need is exposure to my evolutionary systems theory. I accepted, and delivered a series of talks on a world constituted by integral systems on various levels of organization and complexity—including the international.

While at Princeton, I met a member of their faculty, Thomas Kuhn, author of the famous philosophy of science book, *The Structure of Scientific Revolutions*. At lunch in the faculty club, we discussed my evolutionary systems theory as a general theory of evolution in nature and society. I called my theory "GET" (General Evolution Theory), following the example of the GUTs (Grand Unified Theories) discussed by physicists. I suggested that Kuhn's concept of a "paradigm" is likewise a general—or generalizable—concept: it applies to all systems in nature and society, not just to theories in science. He agreed, and encouraged by this finding I began to develop the concept of "paradigm" in a wider, more general sense. This concept caught on, and ever since then has been inspiring my work and the work of other progressive thinkers and scientists.

My talks at Princeton led to an invitation by the recently-founded global think tank known as the Club of Rome. And that in turn led to my work at the United Nations, as director of a program at the UN's Institute of Training and Research (UNITAR). These developments provided the setting for the third humanist-activist stage of my life-journey. But let me not get ahead of myself in recounting my voyage.

At the conclusion of my tenure at Princeton, I published a book that applies evolutionary systems theory to the contemporary world system and its prospects titled, *A Strategy for the Future: The Systems Approach to World Order*. It caught the attention of the founder of the Club of Rome, the Italian businessman and thought-leader, Aurelio Peccei. He asked me to produce a report to the Club on the goals and objectives to pursue in the world system, following up the widely read Club of Rome report, *The Limits to Growth*. This was a major challenge, and I accepted, although I was concerned that I didn't have access to the resources needed to carry it off. Peccei said that this problem can be solved. He called Davidson Nicol, the executive director of UNITAR—the United Nations Institute for Training and Research. Nicol promptly invited me to come to the Institute as a special fellow. This provided me with an office in New York, a secretary and, above all, the means to communicate with nearly any researcher I wanted. (In the era prior to the global information-communication revolution, working for the UN also opened channels of communication that were not otherwise available.)

I moved to New York and worked for the UN for seven years. There, I suggested that the difficulty of the UN to create an effective world system stemmed from the gap between reality and aspirations. Reality is a set of nation-states that consider themselves sovereign and autonomous, co-operating only if they wish; and they wish only if it serves their own perceived interests. The aspiration is to create a functional world-level system coordinated by the United Nations. The leap from the nation-state to the global level is too big. The solution, I argued, was to create an intermediate level of organization, on a regional level.

With the support of then Secretary General Kurt Waldheim, I established a program at UNITAR called "Program on Regional and Interregional Cooperation." It brought together several dozen social and political science institutes in various parts of the world, and was served by a small but dedicated group of mostly young collaborators in New York. At the termination of the program, I had in hand a "Declaration on Regional and Interregional Cooperation" signed by eminent personalities from many parts of the world. It was ready to be communicated by the Secretary General to the General Assembly.

There was, however, a technical glitch: such a proposal could only be "recognized" by the Secretary General if it came from the head of research at the UN system, an under-secretary-general. It so happened that the newly-appointed under-secretary did not want to promote a project that ran under the aegis of his predecessor. The recently appointed Secretary General, Javier Perez de Cuellar, who took over from Waldheim, expressed to me his regrets: he read the Declaration and was ready to endorse it, but due to the failure of the new under-secretary to hand it to him, he could not "recognize" it. In consequence, the Declaration has never been proclaimed. This was not a complete fiasco, however, because many ambassadors to the UN had a copy of the Declaration, and many heads of agencies did, as well. In the following years, the spirit, and sometimes even the letter of the Declaration, found its way to inspire a number of effective measures. Additional treaties and even organizations have been created on the regional and interregional level, and some existing programs have been revitalized.

I left the United Nations and retired to our family retreat in the hills of Tuscany. This was to be a year of repose and renewal, taking a fresh breath and turning over a new leaf. But that "sabbatical year," starting in 1984, did not end even to this day. My sabbatical proved to be an extended period of active and intense work: activism in the interest of creating a better world. I became affiliated with the United Nations University (UNU), headquartered in Tokyo, and offered to set forth my work for the Club of Rome. I suggested important additions to the Club's membership, but its leaders were not inclined to cooperate. I felt that such changes are needed: the one-hundred members of the Club were leading business people and politicians with a smattering of established academics, and they preached to the converted. They did not succeed in creating a real impact on the world's social and political system. New members, closer to the heart of society, were needed.

Given that my attempt to reform the Club of Rome did not succeed, I decided to create a new think tank better adapted to work toward a cooperative and integrally whole world system. I called the new organization The Club of Budapest, bowing to the fact that its organizational meeting was held in that city.

There was a major difference in vision and aspiration between the two clubs. The Club of Rome wished to influence the way the world acts by calling to task its leaders. The Club of Budapest proceeded on the assumption that progress toward a better world called for the active involvement not only of leaders in business and politics, but people close to the heart of society. The requirement was for a club of charismatic people who could touch the mind and the heart of people and address their spirit and consciousness.

In a surprisingly short time, the Club of Budapest succeeded in bringing together the right people. They included H.H. the Dalai Lama, whom I had the privilege to meet and win as a collaborator in drafting the *Manifesto on the Spirit of Planetary Consciousness*; the world-renowned violinist Yehudi Menuhin; the equally renowned Swedish actress Liv Ullman; and the illustrious playwright, actor, and writer Peter Ustinov. Soon, two visionary national presidents joined us, as well: Czech President Vaclav Havel, and Hungarian President Arpad Goncz. The Soviet reformer Mikhail Gorbachev (by then out of office and devoting himself to the humanistic reform of world politics) followed soon thereafter.

The Club of Budapest, as well as the Laszlo Institute of New Paradigm Research, which I founded to research the new paradigm in science and society, are the backbone of this third, humanist-activist stage of my life journey. The Club of Budapest Secretariat is now headed by long-time friend and collaborator Maria Sagi, assisted by an eminent board of curators, and backed by a twenty-four-member international network coordinated by Anne-Marie Voorhoeve. The Laszlo Institute carries out the search for the scientific foundation of the vision of a holistic world guided by the paradigm born at the cutting edge of the sciences. Its young and expert staff is headed by long-time collaborators Alexander Laszlo and Gyorgyi Szabo, together with Kingsley L. Dennis, William Stranger, Giacomo Brucciani and Nora Csiszar, and is advised by eminent personalities such as Emanuel Kuntzelman, Pier Mario Biava, and Riccardo Illy. Christopher Laszlo and the Chinese business leader Frederick Tsao partner the Institute and co-host "New Paradigm Books," a series of studies and articles appearing under its aegis.

Taking Stock

Wonderful people have helped me along my journey, intuitively as well as rationally grasping the mission behind it. Have I lived up to their, and my, expectations—have I come closer to understanding the purpose of life? Sometimes I think I have come closer to it, but the quest is not ended. I need to keep growing with humility in face of the enormity of the task. I must remember Plato's warning: all claims about the real world are at best "likely stories." The question I must ask myself is whether the purpose I have come across in my journey is a likely story. Ultimately, the reader has to be the judge of that.

To help with the assessment of my endeavor, I cite here what I wrote about the purpose of existence in my recent book, *The Wisdom Principles*.[1] This excerpt summarizes as clearly as I can the gist of what I mean by purpose, when it is applied to an issue no less than the purpose of our existence.

> The key to it is the recognition that we are not *biophysical* but *psychophysical* entities. On the one hand, we are bodies: matter-like vibrations in the cosmic field. But on the other, we are mind-like vibrations—intrinsic parts of the consciousness that pervades the universe.
>
> Each of these elements of human life follows its own evolutionary trajectory. Through our body, we *observe* the evolution of matter-like vibrations (material bodies); and through our mind, we *experience* the evolution of mind-like vibrations (our consciousness). We observe that matter-like vibrations, "bodies," evolve toward higher and higher levels of coherence and complexity, and we experience that mind-like vibrations, consciousness, evolve (or can evolve) toward higher and higher levels of development. The higher levels

[1] *The Wisdom Principles: A Handbook of Timeless Truths and Timely Wisdom* (New York: St. Martin's Essentials, 2021. Used by permission of the publisher.

characterize the mindset of mature, "evolved" individuals. They are an awareness of the presence of embracing oneness and unconditional love in the world.

The matter-like and mind-like evolutions unfold simultaneously. They are distinct but not categorically separate: they are processes in the same universe. Evolution in this universe is oriented at the same time toward higher levels of complexity and coherence, and more and more embracing oneness and love.

But what is the purpose of these simultaneously unfolding processes? The answer to this is at the same time the answer to the purpose of life. It is furnished by noting the direction taken by these evolutions. The universal direction taken by evolution is evident throughout the realms of living systems. It is ascension toward higher and higher levels of complexity and coherence in regard to the body, and toward higher and higher levels of oneness and love in regard to the consciousness associated with the body.

The purpose of life, we can conclude, is one, but it manifests in two ways. One of the manifestations of the purpose of life is the evolution of the body—the living organism. This evolution is toward higher and higher forms and levels of coherence. The other manifestation of the purpose of life is the evolution of consciousness: of the mind associated with the living organism. And this evolution is toward higher and higher levels of oneness, and more and more profound and encompassing forms of love.

Lastly, I need to address one more fundamental question—indeed, *the* fundamental question. Is there a "hidden" factor, perhaps a force or a Being, underlying the world we observe?

Let us note that evolution appears to be a universal feature of the universe, and this evolution appears to be nonrandom and, despite numerous bifurcations and temporary halts and reversals, it is enduring and basically unidirectional. This implies the presence of something higher or deeper in the world than simply blind chance, however fortunate it proved to be in producing a coherent universe. What would be that something?

The Abrahamic religions that dominate the spiritual traditions of the West see this something that is beyond the perceived reality of the world as a transcendental Being. It is the Creator, and the world we perceive and inhabit is its creation. Is that the most likely story? That something could also be immanent in the world, as the eastern traditions of Asia and the animistic traditions of Africa see it. Interestingly and importantly, the immanentist vision is now shared in the natural sciences at their cutting edge. The more likely story may be that the something that created our nonrandom universe is a force, a subtle but effective impetus, that biases interactions in a nonrandom direction. I have called this impetus "the holotropic attractor," given that it creates a statistically significant tropism toward coherence through a correspondingly nonrandom series of physical and physical-chemical interactions.

Can we say something about the nature and identity of this attractor? Evidently, in the scientific context, the cosmic attractor is not likely to be a Being—it is more likely to be a non-vectorial, "informational" factor that subtly but effectively orients the universe's nonrandom interactions. Leading scientists including Einstein, Planck, Jung, and Schrödinger recognized the probability of such a factor and called it Mind or Spirit. The most appropriate term for it, I suggest, is *Consciousness*. The randomness-reducing, subtle, but effective, impetus manifesting in the universe is not likely to be an entity, and it is not likely even to be a force (in the sense in which it is defined in physics). The fitting term for identifying it is Mind or Spirit. It is a Cosmic Consciousness that, to use David Bohm's term, "in-forms" effectively, but not physically "forms" interactions in space and time. It in-forms the interactions of our brain and body. In the language of spirituality, it is the divine spark that inspires great works in art and great theories in science. It may be the source of our—and not only my—persistent belief in the purpose of life.

* * *

Questions for Discussion

1. Ervin's quest was fundamentally concerned with finding the purpose that underlies his life and all life. To what extent has a concern for purpose figured in your own journey? How do you understand the relationship between individual purpose and collective purpose? Are they the same or different?

2. As a pianist, Ervin encountered in music an "experience of wholeness and completeness" that stimulated his own philo-sophical investigations. What is the spiritual significance of music and the arts for you and your community? What is it that music communicates that can be so transformative?

3. Ervin's world was transformed when he came to see himself apart of an "interconnected whole." Why do you think this is significant? What is the relationship between independence and interconnection in the spiritual path?

4. Ervin was equally transformed by experiencing the truly fluid nature of reality: "flowing," "treeing," "clouding." What would change if you began to see the world as more fundamentally verb-like, rather than noun-like? Is God better conceived as a verb or a noun?

5. Ervin distinguished God as a transcendent "being" or "entity" from a "cosmic consciousness" immanent in the world. What implications might this distinction hold for your own spiritual journey? Are these distinctions contradictory or complimentary?

Sages to Explore

- B.K. Mallik
- Alfred North Whitehead
- Henry Margenau
- F.S.C. Northrop
- Ludwig von Bertalanffy
- Thomas S. Kuhn

- H.H. the Dalai Lama
- Albert Einstein
- Max Planck
- Erwin Schrödinger
- David Bohm

4: God in the Fullness of Every Moment and Every Thing

Sheri D. Kling

I have often felt like Job. You've probably heard of him—the prover-bial long-suffering and faithful servant of God who was tested by the Adversary with one calamity after another. His friends all insisted that he must have been guilty of something but Job was certain of his innocence. He demanded to meet God in court, and when he got his way, boy, the Lord gave him an earful. But then God acknowledged Job's right to raise his voice and his fists at the heavens and restored everything to him that he had lost.

Though I may not be sitting on an ash heap covered in boils having lost every person and everything of value in my life, I've certainly railed against God over my own suffering and that of the world. I've often felt unfairly treated at the hands of God. Haven't we all?

In my early life, while my family did the best that it could, I expe-rienced trauma at home and bullying at school. Deep fissures grew in my psyche that have affected my life for decades. In his book, *Trauma and the Soul: A Psycho-Spiritual Approach to Human Development and its Interruption*, Donald Kalsched shows how traumatic events in a child's life can cause the psyche to "split" into parts. When the developing psyche is overwhelmed by an experience, it protects itself from complete destruction by tucking pieces of the experience into different aspects of the mind and body. But though the psyche is protected, the person no longer makes sense to herself. My life has been one of slowly weaving the pieces of myself back together again.

As a result, my spiritual journey has long been inter-threaded with my psychological journey. Together they have made a rich tapestry of great depth and vibrant color. Yet, at times, I've yearned for a simpler life. Maybe even a life less "godded." I've even been known to say that I'd trade it all for a good marriage. But marriage has not been my path. At least not yet. Hope does, after all, spring eternal.

The path that I *have* walked has been impregnated by and with God, God-talk, God-think, and what I thought were Godly demands. It's a journey that I might separate into these four phases:

1. God Inside the Church
2. God Beyond the Church
3. God in the Emptiness
4. God in the Fullness of Every Moment and Every Thing

What follows is an account of significant portions of my spiritual journey to find God in the fullness of every moment and every thing.

God Inside the Church

I grew up in New Jersey, and in the Lutheran church, in a branch that eventually came to become the Evangelical Lutheran Church in America, or ELCA. My mother has always sung in the church choir, and I joined the junior choir at the age of nine. Around the same time, I started taking guitar lessons from Mrs. Garcia, the bohemian and very loving teacher who lived just down the street. Folk songs, school glee club, sung liturgies, and church hymns set the meter of my days.

Life in the Lutheran church meant that I heard the word "grace" a lot and the lectionary system it followed meant I learned all the good Bible stories. I treasure the memories of making Advent wreaths, candlelit Christmas Eves, and potluck suppers. I treasure less hearing the murmurs of church politics by the age of twelve when my family left one congregation to join another. Going to church every Sunday was just what I did, even through high school and into college. I wasn't a "Jesus freak," or a "Bible thumper." But singing in church was as much a part of me as was singing in the high school glee club. Music and God as Father, Son, and Holy Spirit was the scaffolding upon which hung my religious world.

So when I moved to the Atlanta area after college, joining a Lutheran church was a natural step. In fact, I became a member of the choir before I was a member of the congregation itself. And I treasured that place. The people loved me, and I loved them. It was true community in every sense of that word.

I adored Pastor Kent whose sermons were intelligent and engaging. I took part in small group ministries where prayer became real. I attended a Cursillo three-day spiritual retreat and learned the languages of both fervor and silence. In that period, my religious education grew by leaps and bounds. I heard a visiting nun use the word "myth" when referring to Genesis and I began reading authors like Marcus Borg, John Shelby Spong, and Henri Nouwen who showed me a new way to understand my faith. I subscribed to *Bible Archeology* magazine and met biblical scholarship that wasn't typically preached in most churches. I also read *Sojourners* and learned about faith, politics, and culture through the lens of social justice.

It is widely acknowledged that when people begin seminary education, their faith is "deconstructed," a process that can be somewhat scary for many as it typically uproots the faith of their family and requires one to build one's own faith. For me, thanks to a wide-ranging reading list, my Christian faith was deconstructed long before I went to seminary. My reading also led to regular theological discussions with Pastor Kent. In one of those, I remember saying that I thought Christianity had become too "Christocentric." I thought we spent too much time worshipping someone we should be following.

And soon I fell in love with the mystics.

God Beyond the Church

The mystics I loved best—from both East and West—spoke of a world that was dripping with God. In their world hazelnuts were holy and dreams and visions brought real encounters with a Serious Sacred who demanded more from us than mere worship. That numinous presence seemed to desire true engagement. My engagement with God suddenly leapt beyond the bounds of the Church into Nature, the new sciences, eastern thought, and mind-body integration.

I became a member of the Institute of Noetic Sciences and discovered a new frontier of consciousness studies, energy medicine, and quantum physics that showed me that our world was way wackier than we like to think. I also read Christian de Quincey, who described consciousness as "going all the way down," and introduced me to philosopher Alfred North Whitehead. Little did I know that his brief mention of Whitehead would presage my future academic career.

In the mid-1990s, a trip to the southwestern United States placed me at the edge of Canyon de Chelly and plunged me into a vision of myself as an infinitesimally small speck of dust in the universe who was intimately connected to *everything*. I *felt* that truth to the core of my being in a vision whose mystical power has never left me even as I've struggled to integrate its meaning into my daily life.

Then Clarissa Pinkola Estes rocked my cosmos with *Women Who Run with the Wolves*, and soon I couldn't get enough of Jungian writers including Robert Johnson and Marion Woodman, or Joseph Campbell and *The Power of Myth*. I dipped my toe in the waters of the East, learning a little of Buddhism, Hinduism, and Islam. And God started speaking to me through the natural world, through my dreams and through head-turning synchronicities where flocks of goldfinches arrived just when I prayed for a "nature moment" to lift my spirits.

I began to feel less and less connected to the label "Christian," mostly because the public face of the faith had become so hell-bent on fundamentalism and political power. But then a book by Joyce Rockwood Hudson called *Natural Spirituality: Recovering the Wisdom Tradition in Christianity* connected Jungian psychology to Christianity in such a compelling way that I knew I had found my footing in the Christian faith again.

For years, my primary psycho-spiritual practices had been journaling and prayer, but now Jungian dream work and observation of synchronicities took center stage. I found a river of wisdom running through my life that was just downstream from God's Wisdom, Sophia, and that sacred flow began to integrate the pieces of my fractured life.

Navigating by that divine current led me to step out in faith as a performing songwriter when I was downsized out of another software marketing job in 2003. It hit me while I was driving my car one day that maybe I was supposed to do more with my music, and the inrushing sense of expansion that I felt from head to toe let me know that this was surely the path of my soul, surely God's call.

Frankly, I was exhilarated when I learned of my impending job loss, because it seemed like the divine kick in the pants that I needed to get on with my authentic life. For the next six years, divine guidance seemed to be everywhere, and I felt God's presence speaking to me through every bush, every dream, and even a butterfly and a highway billboard. I was swimming in the immense power of what Jungians called the "collective unconscious." It was a heady experience and, at times, flirted a little too closely with dangerous ego-inflation.

I followed God's call upon my life. But my dream of making a living through music stalled and after six years I knew I had to do something else. By that time, I had moved to the mountains of northeast Georgia and was living in a charming hundred-year-old farmhouse on eight acres of land where I adopted my beloved dog, Cotton. I felt like the feminine face of God had called me there, confirmed by the presence of a cement Virgin who greeted me as I walked the property for the first time.

I've never loved a landscape or a community of people as much as I loved the Sautee-Nacoochee community in Habersham County, Georgia. It was, and still is, the home of my soul. I believed I'd gone to the hills for discernment, immersing myself in wilderness time to better hear God's call forward. For me, God's call upon Abraham's life wasn't just myth or history but was an archetypal pattern that lays claim to my life today.

Finally, clarity emerged and I felt it was time to honor that fifteen-year tug to pursue theological education. I became a master's student at the Lutheran School of Theology at Chicago. I hadn't planned on going to a Lutheran school, but when I set foot on that campus, it felt like home. The rhythms were familiar and the faces were friendly. And I was drawn into LSTC's coursework in religion and science that included ecological themes.

During orientation, a New Testament professor spoke of a dream he'd had in which humans, animals, birds, and reptiles all came to the rail for communion together; he then told us that he no longer felt his spiritual path was one of ascent, but now was leading him to descend into his own depths. I knew I was in the right place. The dots were being connected yet again.

God in the Emptiness

I've always been one of those people who can't help connecting dots—and so the pattern of integrating multiple disciplines and ways of thinking arises again and again in my life. It was while I was in Chicago that I was finally able to take a course on Whitehead and process theology, and I came alive when I connected his work to that of Carl Jung. The idea that the world was always in the process of becoming and that Christ was the creative transformation available to all spoke to me on a very deep level and seemed to echo Jung's process of individuation. Even more, Whitehead's theory that everything was interconnected and interrelated put my Canyon de Chelly experience into words.

Another set of surprising synchronicities led to my meeting professor Philip Clayton from the Claremont School of Theology. Dr. Clayton took my interests seriously and was one of the most generous scholars I'd encountered. In 2011, after graduating from LSTC, I found myself moving all my earthly possessions to California, so I could pursue a doctorate in religion with a focus on process studies.

There was no question as to what I would research at Claremont. The tug of Whitehead and Jung never weakened, and so I happily continued to study their writing. I was very sure of myself and my direction. But shortly after arriving in Claremont, my life suddenly took another Job-ian turn. With perimenopause grabbing the wheel, the car of my life careened toward one health crisis after another. As I've written in the preface to my book, *A Process Spirituality: Christian and Transreligious Resources for Transformation*,

> I was wracked with depression, anxiety, health issues, self-doubts and relationship woes that were so intense that I lost all footing in the worldview I had held for many years. I had long been wrestling with what I knew was a dying God image—that of a demanding and love-denying father—and questioned whether anything I had ever said or believed about God or dream work or spiritual practice made any sense or was in any way efficacious. I knew I had to reject this putative God, and yet I had no idea what would remain if I did.

It seemed the chickens of my early life were now coming home to roost.

I'd been trying to catch those pesky chickens—to bring those traumatized parts of me together—for decades, but the way I approached the problem was itself the problem. I was laser focused on rooting out whatever it was that was wrong with me so that I could have the life I saw for myself. I've come now to see that my rabid pursuit of self-improvement was just internally directed bullying. I felt like the world had rejected me, and because I thought the world could see something about me that I couldn't, I rejected myself.

I was desperate for change. In the spring of 2009, before I went to Chicago I took a silent retreat at a Benedictine convent in Cullman, Alabama, fully intending to wrestle to the ground those demons that still plagued me.

Just prior to that retreat, a new nature-inspired vision had taken root. I'd told my spiritual director that I wanted to be like a tree—firmly planted in the ground but able to move with the emotional winds that came blowing through life rather than being uprooted by them. She shared two passages from scripture, Psalm 1 and Jeremiah 17:7-8. Both speak of the happiness experienced by those who trust in the Lord: they are like trees planted by streams of water; they are not anxious in years of drought or in seasons of heat. Rather, their leaves never wither, and they always bear prosperous fruit.

I wanted that tree.

The first evening of my retreat, when I returned to my spare room after dinner, I took out my journal, put pen in hand, and prepared for battle. Surely, the rejecting voices that were in hot-breath pursuit at the back of my neck would show themselves. Surely, I would be able to see through those overwhelmingly rejecting faces to the face of God. This is what we did, God and me. We wrestled with troubles through the pouring out of words onto paper.

Not this time. God went completely silent. Crickets.

At first, I was confused. Then I got angry. Really angry. It was only Monday, and I was booked at the convent through Friday. It had cost me something to be there, and I wanted God to show up for me!

"You have till Friday," I told God. "Or we are *done.*" For those who are not used to such prayer language, let me say that I have always believed in honesty in prayer. We see such honesty rewarded in the story of Job, and

I believe God can take it when we shake our fists at the sky and bellow out our rage. God doesn't require any tippy-toe meekness.

Tuesday, I walked around the convent grounds and sat silently in all the beautiful places I could find. God, maddeningly, stayed silent too. Wednesday, I drew the tree of my desire in a mandala with the chakra centers of energy spoken of in Hinduism and yoga rising up through the tree trunk. Still, the heavens remained in radio silence.

By Thursday, I had pretty much given up on God but decided to go to the chapel service. As I waited for it to begin, I was feeling very lonely, thinking about missing my mom and about there being no man in my life. I ached for the bonds of familial love. With emotion rising in my throat, I prayed, "No. Just give me the tree. *I want the tree!*"

The service began with a hymn and then a sister ascended the steps to my left to approach the lectern. First, she read the Jeremiah verse about the tree. Then, she read Psalm 1 about the tree. My heart was greatly lifted by this meaningful coincidence, what Jung would call a synchronicity. Clearly, though, there may not have been an answer to my problem; God and I were *not*, in fact, done.

Around that same time, I had a "big dream" that made a huge impression:

> I have received a foam cooler in the mail that contains large pieces of a hacked-up snake, still writhing. I am horrified and slam the lid on the cooler. "This isn't what I ordered!" I shriek, because I had expected something nice, like a turtle. I think about where I can get rid of it, and finally decide to go back to my old complex (the condominium community in Marietta where I had lived prior to the mountains) and put the cooler in the trash compacter with the mechanism that pushes the trash down into the depths of the dumpster.

Can you see the symbolism?

Snakes are often symbols of transformation and new life because they shed their skins. They are also a symbol of the raw power of unconscious life. I understood my dream to be saying that this transformation stuff wasn't what I expected it to be; it was more threatening and scarier than I'd hoped for when I began the journey. My dream ego just wanted to repress it all into my old, unconscious complexes rather than dealing with this raw life force that confronted me.

That dream led me to research serpent symbology in the ancient near East and its relationship to the Genesis story of the Garden of Eden for my first class at LSTC in the Pentateuch and Wisdom Literature of the Hebrew Bible. I was fascinated by what I discovered. Snakes seemed to pop up everywhere, though, thankfully, not literally.

In 2010, while still in Chicago, I had another snake dream. This dream consisted of only one audio line that said, "You will not be resurrected until you allow yourself to be bitten by the snake." I wasn't as sure about what that meant, and so I set that dream aside for the time being, as I continued my studies in both Chicago and then in Claremont.

Now back to the perimenopause-induced physical and emotional crash.

Life decided to come apart at the seams just as I'd signed up for a class on "Becoming a Public Scholar." I was supposed to be learning how to take a message out to the world, but I no longer had a message. My spiritual life was in a shambles, yet here I was in a PhD program in religion, yet unsure if I even believed in God anymore. I told my classmates that I was "breaking up with God," or at least with the bad-boyfriend-abusive-father-god-image that I had held for so many years.

Here's a question: when theologians spoke of the "death of God," could they have been writing of the death of a shared psychological god image? Jung was often accused of "psychologizing" God, but he knew that God was a *fact* of human experience—a psychological fact.

Jung avoided metaphysical theories about the nature of the universe. As a scientist, he was not willing to make assertions about whether God existed *outside* of the psyche, but he knew for certain that God does exist *in* the human psyche. And since there is a God image in the psyche, Jung believed that there must be an "original" God "behind" that image.

I knew I had to "kill" the toxic god image that had taken hold in my psyche. I just didn't know what, if anything, would replace it. But I did it anyway. I walked away from the love-denying god for whom I was never good enough. And though it felt good to stake my claim of being good enough, there was an eerie quiet where that old image used to live. A dark emptiness. We might even call it an *abyss*. I wondered if my life going forward would be one without faith. For days, I moved through the world in a kind of numbness. I had no idea where to go or what to do next.

Then, one morning I realized that my dreams of the previous two nights had a common theme. In both, I had been bitten by a snake. *You will not be resurrected until you allow yourself to be bitten by the snake.*

I think, as what was said of the Grinch who stole Christmas, that my heart "grew three sizes that day." Just the recollection of those two dreams caused an inrush of a new kind of faith, an imageless faith, a holy Mother Sophia presence that convinced me that there was Something or Someone bigger than me that loved me. And that was enough. It was enough to carry me through the passing of my qualifying exams, the writing and defending of my dissertation, my graduation from Claremont School of Theology, and my subsequent hiring at the University of the South in Sewanee, Tennessee.

God in the Fullness of Every Moment and Every Thing

The dream that drove me back to graduate school was that upon graduation I would find a faculty job and live out the rest of my career in a nice college town as Professor Kling. Unfortunately, the market for faculty jobs in the humanities is abysmal, and so I drew from my strong work experience to land an administrative job at the University of the South, familiarly known as Sewanee. And it wasn't until I lost that job just when the world was on the verge of a pandemic that I dealt creatively with the rejection narrative at the core of my being.

Only three years after starting at Sewanee, budget cuts led to a restructuring that threw me back into the hinterlands. By Christmas 2020, I was wrestling again with loneliness and feelings of rejection around both love and work. I plunged into a dark and familiar story, capturing it all on paper as "objective fact." When I finished writing it all out, I said to myself, "I am so tired of this rejection story."

Some years ago, I wrote a song called "Crack in the Door" about how when it's not honest for me to pray, "God, I'm willing to let that belief go," then I will pray, "God, I'm willing to be willing to let that belief go." And that prayer is enough. Enough to open the crack in the door that let's God come through and for a healing process to begin.

Stating that I was tired of my old story was the crack in the door. That willingness to let my old story go was enough, I believe, to allow a bit of space for God to work in God's creatively transforming way. I have learned that if I keep following the thread of God's process, I know I will be led forward to a new place of health and wholeness.

I am still in that process. I've moved to Florida to be near my parents who are now in their late eighties. I have reinvented myself—yet again—as a theologian, teacher, and songwriter. Being open to the guidance of the Spirit has led me to the directorship of a program of the Center for Process Studies called "Process & Faith," as well as doing other work within the process community while doing a good bit of public teaching. And now, rather than looking for God as a force only outside of myself, I am looking for God inside of me. I seek the same discovery made by St. Catherine of Genoa, who said "My deepest me is God."

I have come to believe that God is in the fullness of every moment and every thing. And that every moment and every thing is held lovingly *within* God. For Whitehead, God initiates every moment of becoming and is the living vitality, the vision for possibility, of that moment. Resonant with Whitehead's description of God at the *beginnings* of every moment of experience, Jung believed God was at the *depths* of experience.

The cosmic and psychic realities described by Whitehead and Jung are, I believe, life-changing perspectives that support the integration of our fragmented lives. This is true especially when their ideas are combined with an embodied spiritual practice like dream work where we can experience for ourselves the call toward wholeness and integration that the Sacred places upon our souls.

We are all and always in the process of becoming, and in every new moment possibilities for novelty and creative transformation arise. In some ways, I might say that, given my early life, it is a miracle that I'm still here today. I am living proof that our lives are not determined by our pasts, though I know how hard it can be to press back against the power of the past.

Being held captive by the past might be fine for a rock, but it is not what God dreams for human beings. I believe we always have the freedom to take a creative step—even if that step is miniscule—toward a new future. I know this must be true for every person because this is the very nature of Big Reality itself, and Big Reality is the same for everyone. Creative transformation and novelty are inherently wired into the structure of life itself; these are not selectively available for the privileged few. And yet, there *is* power and pressure in the past. This we cannot deny.

There is also in life what Whitehead calls "mere wreckage." But God takes in all that we do in the world—every joy, every sorrow, every creative act, every destructive act, every trauma, and every healing—and harmonizes it all into a Peace and a Beauty that is everlastingly holy.

So, unlike the traditional theism that stresses God's transcendence above the world, and unlike traditional deism's "clockwork" God who creates a Universe but then steps away to allow it to run itself, the God that I have come to know is in the fullness of every moment and every thing. This God is in intimate relationship with us, even while being paradoxically impersonal in the laws God has established. I have come to see that while there is cause and effect based on law, there is also that grace of which my Lutheran church still speaks.

Where I differ now from the Church is that I know this grace is not only present in those sacraments that it has deigned appropriate. No, I believe we are swimming in grace, but we can't perceive it, just as the fish doesn't perceive the ocean it's immersed in. That grace flows through the thread of every moment, stitching it up into God's own life, creating a garment of incredible beauty. We live, move, and have our being in an ocean of grace that is, and will always be, a Mystery to us.

In that Sacred Mystery we are never alone. We are never rejected. In that Mystery, we *matter*, we *belong*, and we can *experience positive change*. And we can trust that we are loved, we are loved, *we are loved*.

> Blessed are those who trust in the LORD, whose trust is the LORD. They shall be like a tree planted by water, sending out its roots by the stream. It shall not fear when heat comes, and its leaves shall stay green; in the year of drought it is not anxious, and it does not cease to bear fruit. (Jeremiah 17:7-8, NRSV)

* * *

Questions for Discussion

1. Sheri drew important parallels with the story of Job. To what extent have you or your community also felt like Job? What light does this story cast upon the paradoxes of suffering and disenchantment that are part of the spiritual journey?

2. Sheri's spiritual journey moved through four distinct stages with respect to her image of God. Discuss the differences between these stages and images. Which do you resonate with the most?

3. Sheri drew from both theology and psychology in order to heal the fragmentation of her psyche. What is the relationship between theology and psychology in your own life? Is bad theology related to bad psychology? Can you give some examples?

4. What does Sheri suggest about the "death of God" in light of her

journey? If God is dead, which God? Which images of God have died for you? What image is coming to life?

5. Discuss the rich symbol and metaphor of the "tree" as it relates to Sheri's journey and your own. What is the symbolic relevance of a tree for the spiritual path? What other symbols or metaphors are helpful?

Sages to Explore

- Donald Kalsched
- Marcus Borg
- John Shelby Spong
- Henri Nouwen
- Christian de Quincey
- Alfred North Whitehead
- Carl Jung

- Clarissa Pinkola Estes
- Robert A. Johnson
- Marion Woodman
- Joseph Campbell
- Joyce Rockwood Hudson
- Philip Clayton

5: God's Dream

Rupert Spira

When I was seven, I said to my mother that I thought the world was God's dream and our purpose was to make it as pleasant a dream as possible. Fifty-five years later, I find that I have not changed much, although I express myself in rather more sophisticated terms.

This childhood intuition came unsolicited and, as is often the case, I had to forget it and embark on a great journey to find it again and ground it in my own experience. In the Sufi tradition, there is a story that tells of a man who lived in Baghdad and dreamt of a treasure buried under a house in Cairo. He set out on a great adventure, encountering numerous ordeals on the way, and finally found the house in Cairo that he had seen in his dream. On hearing the dream, the owner of the house responded that just the previous night he had dreamt of a house in Baghdad under which a treasure was buried. The traveller recognized it as his own and, returning home, found the treasure he was seeking that had been buried there all along.

Shortly after that innocent intuition, without knowing it, I too set out, so to speak, for Cairo. I embarked on a great search for the "kingdom of heaven," the realm of eternal peace and happiness, in the world of objective experience. However, in my mid-teens, three events occurred which, in retrospect, were the synchronistic counterpart in the external circumstances of my life to the reawakening of my childhood intuition and the initiation of the return journey.

The first was an experience at age fifteen. While sitting on my bed at boarding school in England shortly after a physics lesson, I became aware that there could be no end to objective knowledge. This was the recognition that the mind's knowledge was, by definition, limited and relative. One could never find closure there. I did not formulate it to myself in these terms at the time; I was simply gripped by the intuitive recognition that there could be no resolution in the mind and by the fear of the abyss that accompanied it. Although I would escape the discomfort of this feeling through normal teenage pursuits, a hairline crack had opened in my world.

Second and shortly after this, I came across the poetry of Sufi mystic, Jalaluddin Rumi, which was perfectly tailored to my early childhood intuition and immediately rekindled it. I seemed to know it without knowing it.

And third, around the same time, I found myself at the Camden Arts Centre in London at the retrospective exhibition commemorating the seventy-fifth birthday of Michael Cardew, one of the founding fathers of the British studio pottery movement. This is not the place to describe in detail the impact this encounter had on my life, but suffice to say, my incipient career as a scientist—I had intended to study medicine or biochemistry—came to an end. This was not an exhibition; it was an initiation. For the first time in my life, I became aware of the transformative power of objects. Little could I have imagined then that, five years later, I would start a two-year apprenticeship with Cardew—the last two years of his life—on his eightieth birthday.

If my love of God was reawakened by the poetry of Rumi, and my love of beauty was initiated by Michael Cardew, it would be two more years before my love of truth would be kindled by the introduction to the nondual tradition of Advaita Vedanta, whose teachings, expressed by the Shankaracharya of north India, Shatananda Saraswati, I studied and practiced under the guidance of Dr. Francis Roles at Colet House in London until his death in 1982.

If these three events introduced a hairline crack into the stability of my worldview, the next event was to irreparably fracture it. For three years I had been deeply in love and in my naivety presumed that nothing could touch the sanctity of this relationship. One evening, shortly after I started my apprenticeship at Michael Cardew's pottery in Cornwall, a three-minute telephone conversation put an end to that romantic dream. Later that night, as I lay in bed reeling with sorrow and confusion, I faced the insanity of seeking happiness through objects, situations, and relationships. I fell asleep that night wondering what, if anything, could be a reliable source of peace and happiness.

I was already interested in these matters, but this event injected new energy into my investigation and practice. I delved into the writings of the Indian sages Ramana Maharshi and Nisargadatta Maharaj, whose clinical and rigorous methods of enquiry I'd been familiar with, but which I now embraced with a passion. However, it was not until I met Francis Lucille in my mid-thirties that the previous twenty years of study and practice would come to fruition.

The first words I ever heard Francis say were, "Meditation is a universal 'yes' to the totality of experience." On the face of it there is nothing remarkable about these words, but such was the conjunction of their clarity and simplicity with the fertile soil of my mind into which they fell, that they precipitated an instant recognition: the very nature of my mind was the aware openness in which everything "lives and moves and has its being."[1]

In our first private conversation later that night, when I lamented that it had taken me so long to have this first recognition—it was twenty years since my first encounter with Rumi's poetry—Francis assured me that the previous years had been the requisite preparation. When he asked how I'd come by my great love of truth, I explained how my mother had introduced me to the Vedantic tradition in my late teens. He replied, "How beautiful, the mother handing her son back to God."

---

[1] New Testament, Acts of the Apostles, 17:28.

Over the thirteen years I spent with Francis, attending several retreats a year and regularly staying with him and his wife Laura in their home, so many ideas that I had read and heard in the Sufi and Vedantic traditions became my lived and felt experience. In addition to Francis's own skillful lines of reason, and experiential approach to the exploration of our true nature and the nature of reality, he also introduced me to the teachings of the Indian sage Atmananda Krishnamenon, which further refined my investigative powers. Over and over, through each of these means and, perhaps above all, through the friendship we shared, I was taken to my true nature of awareness.

*

If we were to distil the essence of all the great religious and spiritual teachings into a single sentence, it might read something like this: the nature of our being is happiness itself, and we share our being with everyone and everything.

Let us start with the first of these two recognitions: happiness is the nature of our being. If happiness is the very nature of our being and our being is obviously always present in our experience, we may wonder why its innate peace and joy are not always felt. The reason is that while we know our own being or self, we do not always know our self or being *clearly*.

It is this lack of clear self-knowledge that is responsible for the veiling of our true nature and its innate peace and happiness. And the reason we do not know our self clearly is because we have lost our essential self in the content of experience, that is, in our thoughts, feelings, sensations, perceptions, activities, and relationships, all of which are temporary and changing. None is fundamental to us. What remains when each of these have been removed from us? The fact of simply being.

Our self or being shines in experience as the knowledge "I am." As such, the knowledge "I am" is our most intimate and familiar experience. However, in most cases, and most of the time, our being is so thoroughly mixed with the content of experience that it no longer shines as the clear knowledge "I am," but as the modified knowledge "I am this," or "I am that."

For instance, if I were to ask you to tell me about yourself, you would probably respond with, "I am a man or a woman of such-and-such an age," "I am a mother or a father," "I am single or married," "I am cold, tired, or lonely," "I am depressed, anxious, or excited," and so on. In each of these statements, the "I am" is present but qualified by a certain age, relationship, sensation, feeling, and so on, just as a screen is temporarily qualified by a movie, or the space of a room by the four walls within which it seems to be contained.

However, if all images are removed from the screen, only the colorless, transparent screen remains which, as such, shares none of the limits of the objects or characters in the movie. If all the objects are removed from a room and the building itself is dismantled, only the unlimited space remains. In fact, nothing happens to the space. It is not suddenly reunited with the vast space of the universe because it was never separate from it to begin with. It is simply relieved of an apparent limitation.

Likewise, when our being is divested of the qualities we seem to acquire from the content of experience, we stand revealed as pure being—unconditioned, unqualified and, as such, unlimited or infinite. Being thus, we cannot even say it is *our* being. Just as space does not belong to the four walls of a room, so being does not belong to, nor is it limited by, the characteristics of a person. As such, we are not a human being; we are *infinite being* temporarily clothed in human experience.

*

Traditionally, infinite being, divested of its personal, limited attributes was referred to as God. However, most people, considering themselves to be temporary, finite, separate selves, conceived God to be vast, impersonal, and other. As such, they forgot that God's being is the very essence of their own being and projected him at an infinite distance from themselves beyond and outside of the world. Thus, the duality of the self and the world grew into a trinity of the self, the world, and God, replacing the intuitive understanding of the unity of being and further alienating people from the felt sense of oneness with everyone and everything.

God is indeed universal and impersonal and yet, at the same time, utterly intimate. The being that shines in each of us as the knowledge "I am" is God's presence. Not God's presence *in us*, for there is no "us," no self, apart from God's infinite, impersonal yet utterly intimate being or self in whom God's being may reside. Nor God the Creator, for nothing other than God's presence is ever created. As the Sufi mystic, Balyani said, God's presence is "every day in a different configuration,"[2] without ever ceasing to be itself and without ever entering into or becoming anything other than itself.

However, to satisfy its intuition of God's being and yet honor its belief in God as a supernatural being at an infinite distance from itself, the apparently separate self or person, entered into a relationship of supplication and devotion to God without realizing that he is the very being of their being and the reality of the world. As a compassionate concession to the apparently temporary, finite self that most people believe themselves to be, such a relationship is legitimate. We could even say it is the highest state that an individual can attain, because it places the individual in the right relationship to the whole. This is beautifully expressed in the following prayer which I first heard in my late-teens and have since recited to myself almost every day:

*

The Shankaracharya's Prayer

Oh my Lord, my whole being is Yourself, and this mind
which has been given to me is Your consort.

---

[2] Ibn Arabi and Awhad al-din Balyani, *Know Yourself: An Explanation of the Oneness of Being,* trans. by Cecilia Twinch (Cheltenham, UK: Beshara Publications, 2011).

The life-force, breath and energy which You have given me
   are your attendants.
My body is the temple in which I worship You.
Whatever I eat or wear or do is all part of the worship which
   I keep on performing at this temple.
Even when this body goes to sleep at night I feel I am in
   union with You.
Whenever I walk, I feel I am going on pilgrimage to You.
Whatever I speak is all in praise of You.
So whatever I do in this world in any way is all aimed at You.
In fact, there is no duality in this life of union with Yourself.

However, at some stage—and perhaps this is the greatest challenge
for one who is on the path of devotion—the very sense of being a devotee, and the idea of the beloved that accompanies it, must be abandoned,
because to consider ourself as a self apart from God's infinite being is
to set ourself up as a second self, and that is blasphemy. At this point it
becomes clear that the self-knowledge that shines in us as the experience
"I am" is God's knowledge of himself.

*

Carl Jung once said of Ramana Maharshi that he was like a white spot
on a white page. His apparently individual being had been so thoroughly
divested of all the qualities and limitations that it had previously acquired
from the content of experience that God's being alone shone in himself,
as himself. That is the highest form of devotion. It is pure love, in which
there is no room for an individual self, let alone an other. It is also the
ultimate knowledge. It is, as such, the recognition in which the paths of
devotion and knowledge unite.

Thus, to take the thought "I am" and allow ourself to be drawn into
its referent is at once the essence of meditation and the highest form of
prayer. It is the direct path to peace and happiness because the separate

self on whose behalf our suffering arises, and around whom it revolves and is maintained, has been extinguished. In fact, it has not been extinguished for it never existed in its own right to begin with. Infinite being has simply been divested of the limitations which thought projected onto it, and, as a result, being stands revealed as it essentially is. As Ramana Maharshi said, "When the 'I' is divested of the 'I' only 'I' remains."

This recognition brings the search for peace and happiness in the world to an end. Even if through force of habit, the belief in separation and the suffering that inevitably attends it occasionally resurfaces, it is quickly outshone in the recognition of the fullness of being. However, while this understanding may assuage the separate self's search for peace and happiness, it does not yet speak to our relationship with the world, that is, with objects and others.

*

From my mid-teens to my mid-thirties, I studied and practiced assiduously in the classical Indian system of Advaita Vedanta, or Nonduality. It was the fullest and most complete explanation of reality I had come across, satisfying me equally at an intellectual and emotional level. It also provided the means to experience the unity of being in spite of the appearance of multiplicity and diversity that the mind superimposes upon it.

However, much as I loved the Vedantic teaching and in spite of my intuitive recognition of its truth, its frequent reference to the illusion of the world troubled me. I understood it intellectually, but I spent most of my waking hours in my studio making objects out of clay. It would be hard to find an earthier profession or one which embraced the apparent materiality of the world more fully, and I was devoted to it. I also lived with my companion whom I loved deeply and was, as such, fully immersed in the joys and tribulations of intimate relationship. In short, I loved objects and valued little above friendship.

Suffice to say that the pursuit of truth, beauty, and love encompassed my life. And yet, while beauty and love seemed entirely compatible, they seemed at odds with truth if allegiance to it necessitated considering the world an illusion.

I struggled with this for many years. Was my work in the studio—preparing materials, making bowls, exploring glaze chemistry, firing a large wood-fired kiln, struggling to earn a living—and the pleasures and pains of intimate relationship all an illusion? At best, I paid lip-service to the idea while my actions betrayed the fact that it was all very real to me. It was not until Francis introduced me to the Tantric tradition of Kashmir Shaivism that this conflict began to resolve.

If the Vedantic and Sufi approaches are pathways *to* God, the Tantric approach is a life *in* God. Through clinical lines of reasoning on the one hand and powerful exercises in introspection involving contemplation and visualization on the other, the beliefs that I still harbored in spite of many years of study and meditation and, more importantly, the corresponding feelings that seemed to validate and substantiate them began to unravel and dissolve.

Of the two, the contemplative exercises in which the experience of the body and the world were progressively surrendered to and permeated by the space of awareness in which they appeared were the more powerful. They seemed to have a dissolving power that rational investigation alone lacked. However, such was the tenacity of my beliefs that had they not first been subjected to the scrutiny of forensic investigation, I'm not sure I would ever have given myself permission to make this deeper exploration of the body and the world. This twin approach of reason and introspection were required to dismantle the edifice of the "matter model," the prevailing materialistic paradigm of our world culture in this era, to which I subscribed in spite of my early introduction to these ideas.

*

At some point it became clear that a simple misunderstanding had prevented me from fully realizing what is meant by the suggestion, found in nearly all the great religious and spiritual traditions, that the world is an illusion and had, as a result, precluded my full embrace of it. I had equated an illusion with something that is *not real*, not understanding that an illusion is something that *is* real but is *not what it appears to be.*

For example, a square circle is not an illusion. It simply cannot exist as an illusory appearance. A mirage in a desert, however, is an illusion. It exists, although it is not what it appears to be. It appears as a pool of water, but it is really a play of light. In other words, all illusions have a reality to them. To assert that something is an illusion is not to deny its reality; it is simply to discredit the veracity of its appearance.

Moreover, an illusion does not conceal its reality. The play of light is not concealed *behind* the appearance of a pool of water. It shines *as that very appearance.* It is the limitations of perception that represent the play of light as a pool of water, which is then further substantiated by our belief that the pool of water is real in its own right.

The illusion itself is not problematic. It is the belief that its appearance is real in its own right that is problematic. Seeing the play of light as a pool of water is neutral, believing it to be a pool of water initiates an endless and frustrating search for water in the desert. It is, as such, not the *appearance* that veils its reality, but the *belief* that the appearance is real in its own right that *seems* to conceal it. That is, it is the belief that there really is a pool of water that prevents us from realizing that we are experiencing a play of light. In the absence of that belief, the same illusory appearance is seen as a play *of its reality.*

Likewise, the illusory appearance of the multiplicity and diversity of the world is not itself problematic. Indeed, it is the only way it is possible to perceive a world. However, it is the belief that the appearance is real in and of itself that is problematic, because it validates and substantiates the sense of separation and the unhappiness and conflict that inevitably attend it. The world is not *what* we see; it is the *way* we see. We are free to allow the multiplicity and diversity of the world to *veil* its reality or to see it as an expression *of* that reality. The world appears in accordance with the beliefs we bring to it. We do not think of the world because it exists; it seems to exist, as such, because of the way we think about it.

The illusion of the world is created by sense perception; the belief that it is real in its own right is established by thought. In other words, perception and conception are the twin powers of the finite mind that generate and substantiate the world as we experience it. This does not imply that the finite mind creates the world. It suggests that the mind renders the world in a manner that is consistent with its own limitations. That is, the reality of the world exists outside, prior to, and independent of the finite mind, but it owes its appearance to the finite mind.

*

Does this mean that all knowledge of the world is mediated through the finite mind as Kant would have us believe, and that we are, therefore, incapable of knowing its reality? It would be so, were it not for one fact of experience. Namely our self. Whatever we are as human beings, we emerge from the whole, from reality, just as a wave emerges from the ocean. Therefore, whatever we essentially are must be of the same nature as the reality of the world, just as the substance of a wave is the same as that of the ocean.

Each of us has the deep intuition that we are one person or one entity, even though our experience consists of a multiplicity and diversity of thoughts, images, sensations, and perceptions. So too we have the intuition that the world is one thing, although it appears as ten thousand things. And what is this one thing that constitutes the world, including ourself?

When we dream at night, our mind divides itself into a dreamed world and the dreamed character that we seem to become, from whose perspective the dreamed world is perceived and which seems, as such, to be other than and separate from itself. And yet on waking we realize that the entire dream was the activity of our mind, which is itself a homogenous and indivisible field of consciousness, albeit a limited one.

We, as human beings, stand in the same relationship to the world as does the dreamed character to the dreamed world. In fact, I suggest that the analogy of the dream is not just an analogy, but a *replica* of the mechanism that takes place one level up, so to speak. In other words, each of us are localizations in the mind of God, in universal consciousness, from whose perspective God perceives its own activity as an outside world from numerous vantage points simultaneously, thereby accounting for our experience of a shared world. The only difference is that universal consciousness localizes itself as *numerous* finite minds—that is, as each of us, including all the animals and whatever other beings may exist—within its own "dream," whereas the finite mind localizes itself as *one* perspective within its own dream.

The world, as such, owes its reality to infinite consciousness, to God's infinite self-aware being, but its appearance to the finite mind through whose agency it is perceived. In other words, the universe is how the activity of God's mind appears from a localized perspective. As such, we as apparent individuals are the eyes through which God perceives the inside of her own mind as an apparently outside world. And just as at no point in an individual's dream does anything other than the dreamer's mind come into existence, so at no point does anything other than God's infinite being come into existence. As it says in the Bhagavad Gita, "That which is never ceases to be, that which is not never comes into existence."[3] In other words, nothing exists! That is, no thing, object, entity, person, or world exists as such. Everyone and everything borrows its apparently independent existence from that which truly is.

This is not a nihilistic statement that denies the reality of the world. On the contrary, it is a life-affirming statement that elevates the reality of the world from an arrangement of inert subatomic particles to the activity of a single reality whose nature is spirit or consciousness. It is, in the filmmaker Pier Paolo Pasolini's words, "to return to reality its original sacred significance."

---

[3] The Bhagavad Gita, 2, 20.

There is just God's infinite self-aware being and its own activity. When its own activity coalesces into the form of thinking and perceiving, and appears, as such, as a finite mind, it refracts its own formless, dimensionless being into time and space, and populates it with the events and objects that constitute our world. A finite mind is, as such, the prismic activity through whose agency the one appears as the many. The unity of being is refracted into an apparent multiplicity and diversity of objects and selves. The infinite appears as the finite, God's mind as the body of the universe. As a multiplicity and diversity of objects and selves, the world is an illusion, but as the dream of God's mind, the activity of consciousness, it is very real.

Every time we experience love or beauty we stand, without necessarily realizing it, divested of the limitations we acquire from human experience, as God's being. The experiences of love and beauty are, as such, God's knowledge of himself. They are interventions in the stream of human experience whereby reality is unveiled and stands revealed to itself as it essentially is. A human being does not, as such, *have* the experience of love or beauty. The experience of love or beauty is the death or dissolution of the apparently separate self and its corresponding object, other or world. Love and beauty are, as such, vertical interventions of reality into the horizontal line of time in which human experience seems to take place. They are the experience through which we pass out of time into eternity. In the experience of love and beauty, the activity of the finite mind ceases to veil its reality and instead shines with it. The world is revealed as the face of God.

If we look inside ourself, discarding everything that is not essential, we are, occasionally, suddenly, but usually gradually, divested of the agitation and sense of lack that we inherit from the mind and the body and taste our true nature of peace and happiness, God's nature. If we look outside ourself and refuse to take the evidence of sense perception at face value, we merge in the experience of love and beauty. We could say that the experience of peace and happiness are the taste of God's presence on the inside, and the experience of love and beauty are the shining of God's presence on the outside. Either way, there is only God's presence—a single, indivisible whole, whose nature is spirit, consciousness, love, beauty, peace, joy—refracting itself through the faculties of the finite mind and appearing to itself, as a result, as the universe, without ever being, becoming or knowing anything other than itself.

Fifty-five years of experience, study, exploration, investigation, meditation, and practice have returned me to my early childhood intuition: The universe is God's dream. It is the activity of a single, infinite, and indivisible whole whose nature is consciousness or love, and we, as temporary localizations of that reality have a sacred duty to think, feel, act, perceive and relate, to the best of our ability, in a manner that is consistent with it. Such a life would be one in which the qualities that are inherent in reality—peace, joy, love, beauty, and truth—and the implications of these qualities—kindness, warmth, justice, compassion, tolerance, and generosity—are communicated, shared, and celebrated in the world.

* * *

Questions for Discussion

1. Rupert pointed to three significant events in his mid-teens that set a certain trajectory in his spiritual path. Were there also key moments in your early life that set you on a particular spiritual path? How do these moments stay with you even today?

2. Rupert spoke of his spiritual path as a "return journey." In what ways might your own path be a journey of return? What have or are you returning to when it comes to thinking about God?

3. Consider Rupert's distinction between the knowledge "I am" and the modified knowledge "I am this" or "I am that." Why is this distinction significant? What do you think would change in your life if you were more concerned with *what you are* rather than with what modifies or qualifies what you are?

4. How does Rupert express the relationship between your being

and God's being? To what extent has a false sense of "separation" between you and God been a factor in your spiritual journey?

5. How does Rupert's analogy of a dreamer and his or her dream cause you to think differently about your relationship to God and God's relationship to the world? If the world really is "God's dream," what does this mean for your life and spiritual practice?

Sages to Explore

- Jalaluddin Rumi
- Michael Cardew
- Shankaracharya
- Shatananda Saraswati
- Francis Roles
- Ramana Maharshi
- Nisargadatta Maharaj
- Francis Lucille
- Atmananda Krishnamenon
- Awhad al-din Balyani

6: In Gratitude for My Teachers

Kabir Helminski

When I reflect on my spiritual journey, I see that at every stage I received help from people who dedicated their lives to the cultivation of spiritual experience, and who generously shared their experience with others who came seeking knowledge and guidance. My story is really their story. The story of our lives is intertwined.

I was about seventeen years old when I left behind religious concepts of penance for sins, earning merits through rituals and sacraments, and being rewarded for dogmatically correct beliefs.

In my late teens, I had experienced certain spiritual openings which caused me to view most of the conventional values and ambitions of 1960s American life as constructs of a consumer culture, a massively programmed artificial reality. Too many people seemed to be living behind masks, with no acknowledgement of who they were behind those masks. I could see no other option but to play along, meeting people where they were.

Of course, there were people whose friendship and love I sought. Otherwise, life would have been absurdly meaningless. It is a blessing that Truth leaks into our hearts even while we are partially asleep. And I would eventually do my share of spiritual experimentation with meditation, mindfulness, and yogic practices.

By the age of twenty, a new universe was beginning to open for me. My first in person exposure to the spiritual path was meeting Baba Ram Dass (Dr. Richard Alpert) at the end of my senior year at Wesleyan University. He had just returned to America after his transformation under the influence of Neem Karoli Baba, a guru he met in India. In many ways this would be the beginning of a spiritual revolution in our culture, and for me it was the beginning of making spiritual practice real. What began with Ram Dass, continued with Suzuki Roshi at the San Francisco Zen Center, and eventually led to an esoteric school of the Fourth Way in New Hampshire which lasted for five years.

During these years, I met a number of highly developed human beings from western and eastern traditions. I imagined that enlightenment was a state of super-awareness, a continual "high," a state of perpetual "non-identification." Not that anyone I met actually embodied that state, but there was the assumption that with enough spiritual practice, which meant sitting still and quiet for long periods, supplemented perhaps by the continual repetition of some mantra, one would either gradually or suddenly attain such a state.

I had seen through the veil of conventional consciousness and had a number of experiences of literally ecstatic bliss and white light. But when, at the age of thirty-two, I met a master of Love, I felt I had come home.

In Perfect Poverty, God Appears

My first encounter with a Sufi *murshid*[1] forever changed my idea of what a spiritual master could be. He could have been someone's grandfather from Sicily, dressed in a three-piece suit, walking with a cane, the bearer of a mischievous yet innocent smile. But somehow, contained within this merely earthly form was a powerful generator of heart-melting love—a love free of any sentimentality, sanctimony, or possessiveness.

I had been used to teachers who cultivated a respectful distance with

---

[1] *Murshid*, a spiritual teacher, literally "one who guides," a spiritually "mature" human being.

their students, preserving that fine edge of awareness that one should bring to the teacher-student relationship. Yes, there was an air of entitlement, of privilege, as if the teacher lived on a different plane of reality, both in public and in private. But with this Ottoman gentleman from Anatolia there was no hint of anything artificial separating us. Suleyman Dede was always ready to go one step further in generosity, service, patience, and affection. When we visited him in Konya, he and his wife, then in their eighties, offered to do our laundry (of course, we didn't let them). If I kissed his hand, he held my head to his chest. If we brought grapes to the home, we left with a watermelon.

From my first steps in the Sufi Path, I heard it said, "It is the human being who matures another human being." Nobody develops themselves in isolation. A fruit tree that has not been pruned will not give the best fruit. Such a tree is not of much use. A dervish is someone who has accepted being pruned and is also being fertilized, cultivated, and looked after. A person who thinks they do not need this cultivation will be unlikely to discover their true identity and will live primarily at the superficial level of their ego, never realizing their true identity.

During the five years we had with our Suleyman Dede, what we learned had less to do with spiritual techniques than acquiring a "taste" for a higher order of reality. The impact was somehow so powerful because it was conveyed both with the metaphors and imagery of Rumi, and with a tangible vibration of ego-melting Love. After each trip to Turkey, we would return to Vermont, subtly and deeply changed, until enough time would pass, and we would want to go back to experience that Love once again, to try to understand what it was, to better be able to live it.

Knowing him did not inspire me to become a scholar of religion or to exercise any sense of ambition in the field of Sufism. He simply inspired me with a sense of inner truth, something which could never be attained without humility and genuine Love. He would say things like, "Mevlana sent me from Turkey to spread his message. I am not doing anything. Allah carried me high above the clouds like Gabriel, across oceans. I am not doing anything."

Dede was never too serious. He would joke about the "huffing and puffing" of Sufi *zhikrs*, about people dressing to look pious, and about westerners and their lack of manners. But he was never sarcastic or mean; it was just an innocent playfulness. On the rare occasions when Dede did get angry, it was never for personal reasons, but from his sense of how people could corrupt religion for their own self-serving purposes.

People sometimes ask me, "What is a Sufi? Can you have Sufism without Islam? Does it predate Islam? Is it something other than Islam?" Well, we've learned there's more than one Islam. What has been most precious is the shift in my perception of reality. Call it a lullaby if you like, or wishful thinking, or even some delusion, but I am convinced now, and more and more every day, that all of existence derives from Love. This loving mercy imbues every particle of existence, and even the events of our lives are purposefully arranged to reveal this Love to us.

Others may experience reality as random, arbitrary, absurd, and even cruel. We acknowledge these bitter truths, too—the devastating griefs and the immeasurable sense of injustice in the world that cannot be denied. But for us, this is not the whole truth, or the highest truth. And nothing that we genuinely experience is apart from the vast context of Love's Universe. Every experience of Life will enrich an individual soul that begins to trust this Love.

Such was the education that began with our *murshid*, Suleyman Dede, in Konya, Turkey. If I touch my forehead to the ground, if the names of God are on my lips, if I strive to bring the words of Rumi (or, as we call him, *mevlana*, "our master") into contemporary poetry in English, it is only in the service of that Love.

Our daughter, Cara, is a painter concentrating on horses and other animals. People are stunned at how she can capture the soul of a horse, kitten, or fox. A few years ago, she decided to paint a portrait of Suleyman Dede as a Christmas present for us. Cara was born some months after Dede had passed from the world and so had never met him as our two older sons had. When she presented the painting to us, she said, "Every time I went to work on this I would weep, and I don't know why." This was exactly the effect he had on people while he was with us in this world. Many times we have gone to his grave in Konya with friends who never had the pleasure of meeting him; so often these friends were deeply moved by the presence experienced there. More than once, I have asked these friends what they were feeling. The answers vary, but are always something like tenderness, humbleness, devotion.

Dede once modestly described himself as "just a faithful dog at the threshold of Mevlana (Rumi)." There's no doubt in my mind that he was a portal for the *baraka*, the living grace of the Path of Rumi and Shams. Shams of Tabriz once said, "The one in whom poverty is complete is the one in whom God appears." Dede was an example of perfect, unpretentious modesty.

In the late summer, when we often visited Konya, wheat would have grown up among the gravestones of the Haji Fattah Cemetery, and after returning to America I would find spikes of wheat stuck to my socks. Years later, I would discover and translate a certain ghazal of Mevlana's that reminds me of this mysterious chain of being, of the grace that poured through Suleyman Dede, Rumi, Shams, and finally Muhammad (peace be upon him). Here is a portion from our book:

Love's Ripening

If wheat sprouts out of my grave,
the bread you make of it will get you drunk.
The baker and the dough will go insane,
and the oven will recite intoxicating verses.
If you come to visit my grave,
my tomb will appear to dance.
O brother! Don't come without a tambourine,
as the sad can't join in God's celebration....
God has created me from Love's wine,
even if death takes me, I am that same Love.

Our connection with Suleyman Dede endured for the last five years of his life, during which he started to lose his capacity for articulate speech. It was evident that his understanding was clear, but forming the connection with words was being lost. Around this time, there was another much-respected elder in our circle of acquaintances. Murray, as he was sometimes called, was the only person to be found in western Canada who could actually read, write, and fully understand Ottoman Turkish (Turkey, pre-1926). He had been discovered and was asked to serve as a translator for Dede. It was destiny, pure and simple, for Murray turned out to be a hidden master, descended from the esoteric aristocracy of Abkhazia (Circassia) and also trained in a Bektashi Lodge in Istanbul during the 1930s. Murray was a hidden Sufi, avoiding adulation, camouflaged sometimes as a carpenter, a café owner, and even occasionally as a fisherman on the high seas. He and his wife Maisie always welcomed me like family, and I was drawn to them by a spiritual fragrance and charisma impossible to conceal.

As it was becoming clear that Dede did not have much longer to live and his ability to communicate was waning, Murat made a proposal: "When Suleyman Dede passes away, there is no one alive in the Mevlevi tradition who can continue your training, especially in the inner work that was once taught in some Sufi tekkes.[2] If you accept, I will continue your training, and you will apply what you learn from me in the Mevlevi tradition." This kind of arrangement has sometimes been necessary where one lineage comes in to help another line to maintain its spiritual authenticity." On our next and final visit with Suleyman Dede in Konya, we asked Dede's permission to receive this training, to which he responded, "Yes, Murat is a great master."

How Beauty Evokes Love

Murat was for some time the owner of a café in Vancouver where I enjoyed being served a cup of frothy Turkish coffee. One stormy afternoon I took refuge in the Istanbul Café, and our conversation began this way.

---

[2] A Sufi lodge where Mevlevi dervishes underwent 1001 days of training. It might include lodging for the Shaikh and his family, as well as rooms for a number of resident dervishes.

"I had an interesting experience last night. I had been listening to some songs by a recently discovered songwriter. As I listened to one song after another, I began to experience a kind of ecstasy, which was all the more extraordinary since I hadn't been in a very good mood to begin with. It seemed that as I listened to this particular sequence of songs, a crescendo was building and deep emotions were stirred. Memories were evoked—powerful recollections of the first stirrings of my own spiritual life, of my father, or a powerful sense of loving many people who were in my life. I wonder why this experience was so powerful—more powerful, in fact, than my spiritual practices, which may leave me with a feeling of wellbeing and calm, but rarely this kind of ecstatic joy. Afterwards, I felt moved to create, to write and compose something myself, to give expression to the beauty I had experienced."

Murat pondered for a moment as if he were about to reveal some secret. "These songs awakened in you a sense of beauty, and beauty evokes Love. We cannot will ourselves to love just by saying, 'I want to love.' But we can, sometimes, be awakened to the vibration of Love by beauty, and, more importantly, we can create more beauty in our lives, and that will be the cause of more Love."

"Well, I'm very curious," I said. "How can we create more beauty? I'm not sure what you mean?"

"Beauty is anything that causes our nervous system to resonate with the energy of Eternal Spirit. Beauty is anything that the five senses and human intelligence perceives as beautiful. We can create beauty in practical ways, both in terms of aesthetics but, even more importantly, in human relationships. We can gradually engender an atmosphere, an environment of beauty and Love. We call this *adab*. Adab is an expression of beauty, and it is how we *do* Love. The wise people of our tradition understood that adab is a process of alchemy, creating a crucible for our transformation. That's what a Sufi lodge, a *tekke*, is meant to be."

"The Sufi lodge is a place where an accelerated transformation is possible, but a tekke is not just a physical place. Most important is the atmosphere created by a community of people in a subtle and conscious relationship. Each dervish must mature to the point where they can awaken a reciprocal exchange of Love with other members of the group."

"So the Sufi process is not just about me becoming more spiritual? You mean I have some responsibility to become part of a system, a community, and to experience myself as part of something larger?"

"Exactly," he said, "and the atmosphere that is created is the remedy for the toxins that exist in human relationships. In this kind of atmosphere, resentment and judgment melt into affection and acceptance. The alchemy of Love will transform the negativity. That negativity is taken for granted in everyday life. It is a beautiful and amazing process, but I'm not sure North Americans can achieve this. What do you think?"

"It's true that we're up against a powerful force. It seems quite unconscious—the compulsion to choose individual independence over community, to retreat from relationship, our impatience with bearing the faults of others. We have little or nothing requiring us to be together. We can always go to another workshop, another teacher, another spiritual event, or imagine we don't need relationships to develop spiritually. We imagine we can do it all ourselves and avoid the challenges, the messiness of human relationships."

"But the work is to transform the ego that thinks like that, the ego that dresses in clever disguises. The ego especially likes to appear as spiritual, to clothe itself in respectable attributes like self-discipline, intellectual attainment, false humility, enlightened personality, sentimentality, and pseudo compassion."

"I want to know what love is—I don't think I understand it at all."

"Think of Love as a resonance, a resonance between the subtle centers (*latifas*) of your own nervous system and the Eternal Spirit (*Ruh*). You can, to some extent, awaken it yourself, but the atmosphere and energy of a loving community create a stronger resonance. That connection allows more Love and beauty to enter into relationships, transforming more and more aspects of ourselves.

"Through this resonance, we will eventually experience moments of ecstatic beauty as if we are living in a mist of beautiful Love that more and more becomes our natural state and who we are. In that Love, the 'me' falls away, and a 'we' remains. This is why Sufis have always organized themselves in this way, and this is why they can achieve so much more than individual practice alone can offer. A current is generated that connects the subtle centers of the heart in communion with the Eternal Creative Spirit, which is the ultimate Beauty. That is why it is called the Beloved and why we are called lovers."

"So what do I have to do next? What's the next step?"

"Now you will return, and return again and again, to the work of doing Love, to practicing the fruits of love, and to creating beauty. You have more souls to love, more songs to write."

*

The years with Murat were a time of intense clarification of both spiritual principles and group dynamics. He insisted on a nearly mathematical precision of language as much as he demonstrated in his life the power of Love in community. Under his influence, I learned and further developed a glossary of spiritual terms in the English language. "Every profession has its own glossary for the specific ways words are used in that profession. A 'blondie' on a commercial fishing boat is a piece of gear, not a woman of a certain color of hair." Under his influence, I continued developing a spiritual vocabulary in English, in addition to the primarily Arabic terms of traditional Sufism.

Some definitions which I owe to him are: *Humility*, our awareness of our dependence on God, and our interdependence with our fellow human beings. *Will*, the capacity for conscious choice, and the attribute which, above all, distinguishes us from other life forms. *Heart*, the totality of subtle, subconscious faculties by which we grasp the Divine reality.

In his view, spiritual maturity is attained in a network of relationships, a community living in a vibration of Love. Group worship is a means through which the vibration of the community and all its members is raised. If a community can come together without the toxins of negativity, without even a slight trace of interpersonal resentment, self-importance, or hypocrisy, the group vibration would naturally be refined and elevated, and so, too, the individuals would naturally come to live in "a mist of love." Murat and his wife Maisie were living examples of hard work and hospitality.

At first, Murat's teaching was very aligned with the Sufism exemplified by Rumi, and Suleyman Dede had honored Murat by recognizing him as a shaikh in the Mevlevi tradition. In fact, Dede wanted Murat to be his successor, but Murat declined this offer because it would to some degree require him to be answerable to a tradition based in Turkey. Murat was more and more realizing that he needed to represent his own ancestral inheritance, a lineage of esoteric kings of which he was the direct heir, even though he had walked away from it all long ago to try to live the life of an ordinary working man.

Murat maintained that his 26,000-year-old ancestral tradition was the root tradition of all authentic spiritual paths. For me, this proposition and certain aspects of his tribal culture were more a colorful "mythology" than a firm belief. I loved him, and I didn't want to leave the teaching and the community over "beliefs" that I did not consider essential to the process of spiritual transformation. Over time, however, this gap would widen, and my skepticism about certain aspects of the tradition would eventually play out.

At this time, I was planning a visit to my brother in Washington, and I had informed my friend James O'Dea, who was Washington director of Amnesty International, that I would be coming. James wrote back to say that Abdul Aziz Said, professor of international relations at American University and a major behind-the-scenes worker for international peace, wanted to meet me, so a meeting was arranged.

It was within minutes of walking into his office that Aziz asked, "Are you free to travel to Damascus? There's someone there you need to meet. He is an Arab ascetic and a great poet."

"Well, I suppose I could. But I have a teacher. Would it be useful?"

"Yes, he would show you an aspect of yourself you haven't seen, and once you've met, you would have a connection beyond distance and time."

The idea of meeting an "Arab ascetic" was not particularly appealing, but the manuscript Dr. Said gave me was deeply esoteric and poetically fascinating. Though we had been to Turkey often, the Arab world was unfamiliar to us. I left Washington without any clear intention to accept this invitation.

Something happened a few days after returning to Vermont. I received a long letter from Murat, the gist of which was: if I felt strongly that my Path was Islamic Sufism, I was free to leave and pursue that Path. I knew that my path would not be Murat's ancestral tradition, but I had never thought of leaving him. He was now giving me permission. The synchronicity of the invitation I had just received from Abdul Aziz became apparent, and several months later, Camille and I would travel to Damascus, Syria.

The Seven Rivers of Damascus

I vividly remember my first impression of Asad Ali as he received us at the door to his library. This "Arab ascetic" was dressed in a stylish white suit and greeted us with a broad smile and a flamboyant "Salaam! Salaam!" We were about to enter a new world of spiritual refinement, cultivated meaning, and spirited conversation. It is said that the high art of the Arab is rhetoric, and in Damascus we witnessed a love of language and mystical discourse beyond anything we had so far experienced. I can trace some of my most important realizations, or understandings, to that first week.

Dr. Ali said to us one night, "Did you know that Damascus has seven great rivers?"

"No," I said.

"Yes, you don't know them because they're not seen. They're underground," he said playfully. Those seven rivers were the seven states of consciousness, the seven levels of spiritual awareness that the spiritual wayfarer might experience.

In the usual map of the spiritual journey according to traditional Sufism, the soul passes through seven stages of transformation—from heedlessness, to conscience, to presence, to tranquility, and finally to purity and freedom.

Asad Ali introduced an important nuance. Allah, who is Absolute Love, is in love with the self, and from that perspective the essential self of the human being is the beloved. Spirit loves human self-hood, because it is through the self that all the Divine Attributes and Qualities can be manifested in the world. And the human self is meant to love Spirit because everything that is valuable and beautiful in the human being is sourced in Spirit. If the self loves only itself, apart from God, that is a sub-human state. That is what is meant by hell.

That first week was also our introduction to the esoteric dimension of the Qur'an. Dr. Ali lived and breathed the Qur'an and its linguistics. Everything in life, in the world, was but a reflection of the Qur'an, its vocabulary, and syntax.

I brought certain questions about the Qur'an that had been troubling me, and one was, "Why does God say in the Qur'an that the human being is created from a 'blood clot,' or in some translations, simply 'clot.'" I was quoting the first words revealed to Prophet Muhammad (peace be upon him) as commonly translated into English.

"Created from what! A clot? No, no," he exclaimed. "Created from *alaq*. This is the geometry of life, not a clot! *Alaqa* means to reach, connect to, form a relationship with something. Alaq is a clinging substance, you might say, something that intertwines," and he clasped the fingers of both hands to demonstrate.

"Ah, you mean like DNA?"

"Yes, for instance. And more! Allah is continually connecting, proportioning the circumstances of our lives."

It was that first week in Damascus that I began to dream in Arabic, a language I hardly knew, and my dream was a linguistic one, involving two separate but similar-sounding phrases.

> *Mutlaq kitab alayk*
>
> مطلق كتاب لك
>
> *Mutlaq qutub alaq*
>
> علق قطب مطلق

These could be translated as:

> The absolute book for you.
> The Absolute. The spiritual pole, or axis. The germ cell of life.

I understood the first phrase to mean that, while I was a publisher at that point in my life, and a writer with only one short book of Rumi translations published in my name, that here I was being introduced to the Absolute Book, *the Mother of the Book*, as the Qur'an is called.

The second phrase was a cosmological key: God, the Absolute, is brought into the world through a spiritual axis that runs through all levels of existence, right down to the germ of life, *alaq*, which epitomizes the care with which the Divine tends to every detail of life.

Every day of that week was filled with profound insights, high spirits, and laughter. I smiled so much my cheeks began to hurt. More than any meaning or content that I could name from that first week, in Asad Ali's presence we were revitalized with a new energy. I felt I'd been taken by the Divine Hand and put back on the Path I belonged to. For my wife Camille, on the other hand, over the next year poems filled with love and ecstasy flowed through her non-stop—like Rumi after meeting his beloved companion and mentor Shams of Tabriz.

From Syria, we went to Turkey where it seemed doors were opened to us everywhere. For the five years after Suleyman Dede's passing, we had not been back to Turkey but had focused on our training with

Murat. Now we were not only received back in the country which had been the origin of our Sufi connection, but we were being introduced to new friends and connections who would become colleagues, friends, and guides essential in this next phase of our spiritual journey.

And over the coming years, there would be occasions when the home of Mawlana Asad Ali would be the threshold where the two worlds meet. Our closeness with him would continue up to this day, even during the unfolding tragedies that have descended on our beloved Syria.

I remember one very late warm summer night as we sat among the trellised jasmine vines on Asad Ali's terrace. He seemed to go into an altered state and with eyes closed said in Arabic, "Name a Prophet." I was startled but spontaneously replied, "Seth."

Dr. Ali didn't seem to recognize what I was saying until one of the friends said, "Sheeth, Mawlana, Sheeth (the Arabic name for Seth)."

"Azim (great)! It is Sheeth speaking to you."

At the time I knew almost nothing about Seth. Now, who is this figure in the esoteric tradition of Islam? Seth is a Prophet like his father Adam, so he is one of the exalted antediluvian patriarchs of the Generations of Adam. Seth transfers God's Law to humankind after the death of Adam. For clarification, we do not understand the "Prophet" Adam through a Creationist lens, but rather as the first truly conscious human being. Some sources say that Seth was the receiver of revelation, and the revelations he received are said to be the "ancient scrolls" mentioned in Quran 87:18. Medieval historian and exegete al-Tabari and other scholars say that Seth buried his father Adam along with secret texts in the tomb, which tradition calls "the Cave of Treasures."

And so, Mawlana Asad Ali recited the following words which two friends, who seemed to be prepared for such a moment, readily transcribed.

> They are the generous ones, and their fragrance spreads
> through generosity—
> The incense of the Pleiades, a melody of essence.

Greetings from my Father (Adam); and my Mother (Eve)
    sends her sunlight,
To bring together with the intimacy of lights, the Arabs and
    the non-Arabs.

O descendant, the Song of Seth, as you see,
Has renewed rhythm, played on the harp strings of a breeze.

Glory be to my Lord, I wrote the song repeatedly with my tears,
So that the desert smiles and becomes verdant.

My father is Adam, and his new descendants are still born
    among you,
Through Moses and the Master of the Cave, and the wind is
    still alert.

The breeze carries our yearning and greetings for you,
As if Love is being interpreted for the sake of nations.

I love my father and mother, and I speak of spiritual law,
and throne, and footstool, and the movement of the Pen.[3]

The highest morals are those of Muhammad, and his family
    members
Are like flying flags, and happy is the one who catches this
    scent.

Is it enough and would they be satisfied with my greetings,
And the greetings of those who prayed to spare them the pain
    with the Love I have?

---

[3] These are cosmological symbols signifying levels of unmanifest and manifest Being.

The vines of the cluster of talents are bestowed.

They are generous ones, and the fragrance spreads through
　　generosity.

Receiving this message in the form of a poem from the Prophet Seth, so close to the origins of our human race, was like a confirmation of being received into a relationship with the primordial religion of humanity. It has oriented me ever since to the Source of Life, the Sustainer of our consciousness and Love, a unified field of continuous Presence. In subtle stages I awoke and began to see that my life was not mine, but that I belonged to Life itself. My will was not entirely *my* will but an instrument in a symphony that I began to hear. The music was sometimes poignant, sometimes powerfully joyous.

I stopped believing in a God, because believing is less than perceiving, and "God," while not to be denied, is nevertheless a concept open to infinite levels of understanding. As a human being matures spiritually, one's concept of God changes. Yunus Emre, the greatest Turkish mystical poet, looking toward our Origin, sang, "This whole universe is created from a single spark of Love." And Murat, looking in another direction, used to say, "God is the subtlest state of everything."

The image of God we hold can bring us nearer to the Divine, or alienate us from the Divine. The value of our concept of God is that it can have practical consequences to our relationship with God.

Imagine a non-dimensional point located in the core of one's being. That point is the portal to all qualities, energies, and virtues that a human might value. Within ourselves is a window to the Divine through which generosity, courage, forgiveness, and love can flow into us and manifest in our relationships and lives. You and I have not created these qualities. We did not create compassion, consciousness, or conscience. These are sourced in a dimension beyond material existence, and we can reflect these qualities if we have polished the mirror of our own being. We are nothing but reflectors, and yet the subtlety and depth of what a human being can reflect is miraculous. Spiritual development is increasing our capacity to reflect these qualities that are inherent, but latent, in Reality. It is for human beings to cooperate with the Divine to bring these latent qualities into manifestation.

Can a human being ever attain full knowledge of the Absolute? I don't know, but the living presence within the breath, the consciousness that arises from within the heart, the Love that appears inexplicably in this imperfect world when one soul touches another—these point to Something beyond all desires and ambitions, beyond all the sorrows and conflicts.

This unified field of intelligence is always communicating, educating, inspiring. In this self-reflective universe, Love is always seeking to be known, to manifest Itself to Itself in the conscious heart of a human being.

As a practical matter, I aspire to a simple principle: to keep the Friend as my companion in every state.

* * *

Questions for Discussion

1. Kabir's spiritual journey is rooted in a profound gratitude for the relationships that made it possible. In what ways is your own spiritual path relationally grounded? Who are those mentors, teachers, and friends who have shaped you? What have you learned from them?

2. Love is at the heat of Kabir's Sufi path, but love is no simple matter. What is love? What does love involve, and what are its characteristics? Have you experienced the "alchemy of love" in your own life? What do you think is meant by this language?

3. To what extend do you also have, or need to develop, a "spiritual vocabulary"? What is the value of a common spiritual language in binding together a spiritual community? Can you give some examples of your own spiritual lexicon?

4. Consider Kabir's and Murat's discussion of love and beauty. What is beauty and how is it related to love? What might change in your spiritual journey if you not only *understood* this relationship, but also *experienced* and *practiced* it?

5. Kabir came to understand that "the image of God we hold can bring us nearer to the Divine, or alienate us from the Divine." What does he mean by this? What sort of practical consequences does your *concept* of God have for your *relationship* with God? What happens when we forget that our "image" or "concept" of God is just that—an image and concept?

Sages to Explore

- Baba Ram Dass
- Neem Karoli Baba
- Shunryū Suzuki Roshi
- Suleyman Dede
- Jalaluddin Rumi
- Shams of Tabriz
- Abdul Aziz Said
- Prophet Muhammad
- Al-Tabari

7: My Walking the Entangled Ways of Sage, Seer, and Shaman

Jude Currivan

When I was four years old, I had my first experience of realities beyond this realm of existence. I watched while a discarnate light appeared in the upper corner of my bedroom. Although curious, I wasn't scared and was perhaps too young to consider or now recall its semblance as being "other-worldly." In the months and years that followed, through clairvoyant, clairaudient, and clairsentient seeing, hearing, and sensing, I became progressively aware of, and engaged with, the ongoing presence of the same being. I'd come to know this being as Thoth, the ancient Egyptian *neter* of wisdom, alongside other discarnate archetypal intelligences and entities.

Intuitively sensing the benevolence of the connections and the meaningful in-formation that was being communicated, I became able to access insights and guidance that were offered, but never imposed. I increasingly appreciated the empowerment of knowledge and understanding that I was able, in many instances, to later validate and which has, I feel, also added immeasurably to my well-being ever since.

Alongside my "walking between worlds," however, I've been fascinated with how the multidimensional realities I continue to experience interconnect with my very human life. From those early steps, my explorations, through studies of ancient and indigenous wisdom teachings of many traditions, and of the leading edge of scientific investigations across numerous fields of research, and at all scales of existence, have naturally interwoven with and reflected the experiential grounding of my ongoing inner and outer journey of discovery.

Along every step of the way, I've never encountered a sense of separation. Instead, my awareness has been of an ultimately unified, yet diversified Cosmos where, as the Chinese *I Ching* tells: "In the beginning is the One, the One becomes two, the two becomes three and from the three, ten thousand things are born."

I've had a lived perspective of the unified nature of reality from a young age, perceiving multidimensional "spiritual" realms, alongside mental, emotional and physical levels of embodiment. My dear friend and evolutionary biologist Elisabet Sahtouris describes these as different "notes" along an entire piano keyboard of consciousness. Hence, rather than considering such realms apart, I've sought to integrate and manifest them wholistically as attributes of my individuated personal and transcendental awareness of unitive consciousness.

Some years ago, on a clear bright morning near the ancient Neolithic monuments of Avebury in the English countryside, where I've lived for nearly three decades, I heard this clairaudient message: "In the commonality of our humanity, we're all ordinary; in the commonality of our divinity, we're all extraordinary." This I feel sums up the essence of my own and perhaps all our ongoing journeys.

As I'll return to below, despite my experiential understanding of unified reality, my journey would also, and perhaps most importantly of all, teach me not only what it means to be humanly fallible, fearful, and at times forlorn, but also how to perceive and appreciate the parallax between such loneliness and an ongoing path toward empowered aloneness and ultimate all-oneness in a co-creative and evolutionary universe.

*

In seeking to understand the nature of reality and our place in the cosmos, I've noted that there seem to have been three main paths of discovery. I call them the ways of the sage, the seer, and the shaman.

I understand the way of the sage as a mind-based approach to gain knowledge and understanding. Such paths include the wisdom teachings of ancient Egypt, the name for which, *Al-khem*, meaning the black land and referring to its richness after the annual Nile flooding, is thought to have given rise to the term alchemy. Its path involves the purification and perfection of matter and, at its deeper philosophical aim, it has to do with the self and cosmic awareness.

A later follower of this tradition was Isaac Newton, whose writings were predominantly about such esoteric matters. He has sometimes been called the last of the alchemists. Elsewhere in the Levant, and primarily what is now Iran and Iraq, there were followers of Zoroastrian and earlier teachings. These wise men, or magi, gave rise to the word magic, which emphasized links between the power of co-creative intention and manifestation in multidimensional and interconnected realities. Later, the Platonic and Pythagorean mathematicians and geometers of ancient Greece would add their own insights to the burgeoning of a science that viewed the world as whole and inherently sacred, and whose numerically harmonic and geometrically relational appearance emerged from deeper ideational realms.

Over the *longue duree* following the fall of their societies, these perennial wisdom teachings nonetheless endured and, by medieval times, some had been encapsulated in the fourfold teachings known as the Quadrivium. Founded on a perspective of the idealistic and archetypal nature of Numbers, the Quadrivium deemed numbers in space as geometry, and numbers in time as music in a harmoniously interrelated universe.

Another thread of such sacred science is based on a set of mystical texts known as the *Hermetica*, named after the Greek deity Hermes Trismegistus, or thrice-wise, a legendary combination of the Greek Hermes and Thoth. Its philosophical teachings that God is both the All and the creator of the All; the creative impulse and all that is created, both transcendent and imminent, beyond form and meaningfully in-formed, deeply resonates with me.

The other tradition that continues to guide me is that of the Vedic sages of ancient India, whose writings on the nature of reality, the Upanishads, and especially the *Ishavasya* commentary are for me some of the most profound and distilled commentaries on the nature of reality and the primacy of consciousness. In resonances with my own journey, they assert the perspective that mind and consciousness aren't what we *have* but what we and the whole world *are*.

*

From an early age, my fascination for how cosmic mind, God, the All, created our universe, while founded on a great respect for such wisdom, also wanted to see to what extent the last three centuries of modern scientific endeavor had expanded upon its tenets. To my shock, I soon realized that it hadn't. Instead, the perennial philosophy that I found to have such resonances with my own experiences and explorations, was effectively ignored and even derided.

Yet, I could already see that the two pillars of twentieth-century science, quantum and relativity theories, held significant insights into such a deeper awareness. Some early quantum theorists and significantly, Max Planck and Erwin Schrödinger, maintained the primacy of consciousness. And Albert Einstein, by integrating the relativities of space and time into invariant space-time, and by revealing the equivalence of energy and matter as energy-matter, showed how light weaves the realized appearance of our unified universe.

While I was growing up, modern science was also struggling with a foundational question of whether our universe is infinite and eternal, or whether it had come into being at some time in the distant past. Cosmologists eventually settled the question and determined that it began an estimated 13.8 billion years ago, in what Fred Hoyle, who was a leading voice for the alternate, eternal or steady-state theory at the time, called the "Big Bang."

Undeterred, in the early 1970s, I studied physics at Oxford University with the final year of my master's degree. I specialized in quantum physics and cosmology. Fortunately, I met and was mentored by the great Dennis Sciama, who introduced me to the notion of black holes which, at the time, went from being considered only a theoretical possibility, to be considered a surprising reality. It was Dennis who suggested I write on the subject, with which I entered, and won, a university essay competition. It was also Dennis to whom I went with the conundrums posed by what I was being taught, which had no place for ancient wisdom or consciousness. While he offered no easy resolutions, he encouraged me to keep searching and, with a sense of his ongoing support, I've continued to do so.

In the half century since, and further building on profound insights by David Bohm and others, a confluence of theoretical foundations has come together in an emergent and wholistic cosmological framework which is backed up by increasingly compelling and wide-ranging evidence.

Founded on quantum and relativistic physics, which describe the appearance of energy-matter and space-time respectively, this evidence points to our universe in its totality as emergent phenomena of more fundamental nonphysical and causative realms of cosmic intelligence and unified reality.

Converging with the perennial wisdom teachings I've mentioned, the primacy of mind and consciousness, is now being scientifically revealed as being fundamental to the nature of reality. Evermore discoveries are showing that cosmic mind, articulated as a universal "alphabet" of 1s and 0s of digitized information, and crucially combined and expressed as meaningful in-formation, literally in-forms the formation of our entire universe and in complementary ways as energy-matter and as space-time.

Study of the thermodynamics of black holes shows that their informational content is actually proportional to the 2-D spherical surface area of their event horizons rather than their 3-D volume. This is exactly akin to a hologram, where the 3-D appearance of an original object is recreated by projected light from a 2-D surface embedded with its previously gathered 3-D in-formational content.

Expanding this understanding to the appearance of our universe, the so-called holographic principle posits a holographic projection of such meaningful in-formation; literally a cosmic hologram with the projection screen, the holographic boundary of the appearance of space and the projectionist the creative impulse of our universe and all that is created in its great evolutionary manifestation of meaning and purpose.

A further and integrative insight into the key role of the laws of thermodynamics offered me a personal and vital "Aha!" moment that I call a new IN-SCIght of IN-formational SCIence. It occurred to me during the writing of my 2017 book, *The Cosmic Hologram: In-formation at the Center of Creation*, when I awoke at four in the morning, having experienced a profound vision/dream.

I sensed myself standing in the present moment at the bow wave of the expansion of universal space and the flow of universal time. I perceived the incredible simplicity of how the cosmic mind of God realizes our universe as an unfolding and evolving "great thought"—to paraphrase the eminent scientist Sir James Jeans.

I saw how, for our entire universe, the physical principles known as the first two laws of thermodynamics respectively describe the complementary expressions of universally conserved and quantized energy-matter and entropic space-time. And I saw in an instant how expanding their definitions in terms of in-formation, shows how our universe exists and evolves as a unified and nonlocally interconnected entity. Along the way, with quantum and relativity theories also describing energy-matter and space-time respectively, such a thermodynamic-infodynamic complementarity and expansion, also points to how to reconcile these two hitherto unresolved pillars of science.

Two more associated insights came forward, both of which are fundamental to this emergent and integral cosmological framework.

The first relates to the concept of entropy as enshrined in the second law of thermodynamics, which states that the entropy of a contained system (such as our universe) increases over time. The concept of entropy is widely misunderstood as being a system's process over time from order to disorder. A consequential misperception is that open and dissipative subsystems, such as biological organisms, existing in dynamic states and far from equilibrium, somehow reverse this entropic trend and instill localized order during their lifetimes. Such views, I would propose, are fundamentally flawed.

Instead, entropy is actually a measure of the energetic microstates of a system, which do indeed inexorably increase through time. When expanded, as is progressively the case, and representing the in-formational content of a system (with both described by the same equation), which I term "intropy," it too always increases over time. Crucially, the evidence that our universe is entirely pervaded by meaningful in-formation, extends the concept of intropy further still to "in-tropy."

With our universe, having been shown by cosmologists to have begun in its lowest and simplest in-tropic state, as for the more limited notion of entropy, its in-tropy too can only increase through time. Indeed, the ongoing accumulation of universal in-tropy as the holographic boundary of space expands to accommodate its in-formational content, *is* literally the one-way flow of time within our Universe. Ensuring an inherent causality within space-time, its unfolding process thus enables a unidirectional flow of in-formationally guided, co-creative evolution from simplicity to complexity.

The pioneers of the holographic principle, appreciated that its premise of universal digitized information is pixelated at the minute levels of the so-called Planck scale of space and time. In addition to space-time, the Planck scale also reveals universal measures for energy, matter, and temperature, the last as described in the third and final law of thermodynamics.

The other further insight that came forward in my early morning vision was a sudden appreciation that, in the contained system of our universe, and with its entire energy-matter being universally conserved, its in-tropy is inversely proportional to its temperature. This provided a mechanism to drive a perfect cyclic process for a universe that began in a miniscule, incredibly hot, yet ordered state and then cooled down. Space expanding and time flowing ever since has meant that with its universal temperature continuously falling, the in-tropic in-formational content of our Universe has inversely and inexorably increased and so evolved.

Cosmological discoveries have indeed shown that our universe was exquisitely ordered and its laws of physics incredibly fine-tuned from its beginning—emerging not in the implied chaos of a big bang but more akin to the first moment of an ongoing big breath, as again described by ancient Vedic wisdom. In doing so, and considering its fundamental nature as made up of meaningful in-formation, it embodies an inherent evolutionary impulse from simplicity to complexity and ever greater levels of diverse self-awareness. It exists *to* evolve. And as microcosmic co-creators of its innate intelligence, I suggest that we are part of its innate impulse to evolve and embody such a vital purpose at this pivotal moment for ourselves and for our planetary home.

The mathematical signatures of its universally relational and dynamic in-formational and holographic patterns and processes are now being discovered from cosmology, physics, and chemistry, to biology and complex systems. Their harmonic so-called power laws and their self-similar patterns, known as fractals, extend from individual atoms to vast galactic clusters and the relic of radiation or cosmic microwave background

(CMB) that fills all of space. Crucially, such relationships are being uncovered not only throughout the "natural" world but also through our collective human behaviors. For example, the in-formational interplays of internet traffic, website links, and data routes, all embody the same fractal patterns as do biological ecosystems.

A key theoretical prediction of Quantum theory that's also naturally encompassed by this emergent whole-worldview is universal non-locality—an innate interconnectedness in the foundations of reality that transcends the limits of space and time. Crucially, the simultaneous correlations and connections that nonlocality reveals, don't allow any information to be passed within space-time traveling faster than the cosmic speed-limit of light, thus preserving the "arrow" of universal time and its innate causality.

Until recent years, mainstream science generally considered such nonlocality to be only exhibited at minute quantum scales and under specific circumstances of particle entanglement, where "twin" particles are simultaneously connected with no signal passing between them. Latterly, however, such a view has become untenable, with laboratory experiments demonstrating nonlocal entanglement at scales far larger than the quantum, currently to the sizes of organic molecules and even small diamonds.

In 2018, a team of experimenters at MIT went much further. Nonlocally entangling photons of light in their laboratory with starlight from 600 light years away, and with the entanglement triggered by light from two vastly more distant quasars 7.8 and 12.2 billion light years away, they were able to demonstrate such nonlocality, as theoretically predicted, at cosmological scales.

Significantly, such universal nonlocality supports our in-formational access to transcendent awareness relating to so-called supernormal phenomena. Regardless, of whether we're on a spiritual path or not, our being able to experience such expanded perceptions of reality through nonlocal phenomena, including synchronicities, intuitive insights, telepathy, and remote viewing is, for me, a portent and promise of our conscious evolution.

*

While my own path sought to follow the way of the sage, my journey has also melded this path with the way of the seer, with direct experience of mystical and visionary realms and the profound insights they've afforded me throughout. Indeed, in many instances, further progress in my understanding of the nature of reality has been initiated by such seeing and sensing, as has also been the case for many others.

In recent years, the multidimensional and ultimately unified nature of reality is being re-discovered and acknowledged, by ever-increasing scientific evidence revealed by numerous researchers and across many fields. In doing so, the insights of perennial wisdom traditions relating to its innately harmonic and geometrical nature, are being extended and expanded through the perspective of its holographic and meaningfully in-formed expression.

A third path of perception, vitally experienced and embodied in relationship with the web of life, is that of the shaman. For me, while the path of the sage and seer have engaged my mind with a gnosis of revelatory experience, it's the path of the shaman, onto which I first stepped after many years of emotional imprisonment, that broke, freed, and then healed my heart.

In journeying to over eighty countries around the world, I've been very fortunate to learn from and work alongside Indigenous wisdom keepers from many communities and cultures. All have guided and encouraged my evermore profound respect and awe for our planetary home. It was my first visit to Peru over twenty years ago, meeting with the Q'ero shamans there, and inspired by their profound and heart-centered relationship with Mother Earth, that fully awoke a lived love within me.

By then, I'd lived in the sacred landscape of Avebury for five years.

Without yet appreciating that they were preparatory for shamanic initiations, my seer experiences had begun to include encounters with ancestors, plant sentiences, and archetypal intelligences of Earth, Water, Air, and Fire. While such relationships were flourishing and greatly valued, by then my personal and emotional life had reached a point of unsustainability and breakdown.

Through the next year of turmoil and loss, I also slowly found further solace, liberation, and eventual healing by being in nature, discovering joy and feeling gratitude in the changing seasons and the abundance of life that surrounded me. Such was the day-by-day unfolding of joyful encounters such that, by the time I left for Peru, I was open and trusting of whatever might unfold there and beyond.

Empty of expectation, the journey became an ongoing and deepening shamanic immersion; at its culmination, as I stepped onto the shore of Lake Titicaca after a journey on its waters, the beautiful simplicity of a perfectly heart-shaped pebble at my feet caught my eye. In its serene presence, I suddenly glimpsed with visionary wonder its own journey to this place and this moment, and the vastness of our Universe embodied in it.

Overwhelmed with reverence and love, since that day, my onward journey has interwoven and progressively integrated the three ways of sage, seer, and shaman.

My ongoing quest is to continue to deepen my understanding, experiencing, and embodying of unity awareness of an infinite, eternal cosmos and its multidimensional co-creation of our universe as a great thought that exists and evolves as a unified entity. Indeed, ever since that transformational moment, I've been increasingly appreciative of that universal embodiment of an inherent evolutionary impulse, existing *to* evolve from simplicity to complexity and individuated self-awareness.

In the years that followed, I undertook a thirteen-journey pilgrimage around the world and subsequently shared my inner and outer experiences and insights in two books; *The 13ᵗʰ Step* and *The 8ᵗʰ Chakra*. I also managed, at the same time, to complete a PhD in archaeology, researching ancient cosmologies, their cultural paths of sage, seer, and shaman and their monumental expressions.

Some years before, I'd come across researcher James Lovelock's concept of the Earth, or Gaia, as the ancient Greeks called the Earth goddess, as a self-regulating system. I now entered a much more profound and continually developing relationship of living love and gratitude for Gaia as a sentient being. In the more than two decades since that encounter on the shoreline, which I now realize was the initiatory threshold between the before and after of my relationship with her, I've come to term all the aspects of Gaia's evolutionary perception and being, her geosphere, hydrosphere, atmosphere, and biosphere, as a coherent and wholistic *gaiasphere*.

The shamanic way for me is embodied in an everyday love and gratitude for the extraordinary beauty and abundance of her entire gaiasphere and indeed beyond, as embodied in the cosmic trinity of her relationship with our Sun and Moon. I've been hugely fortunate in having the opportunity of experiencing many of her magnificent marvels, including majestic mountain ranges, vast deserts, prolific rainforests, high plateaus, grand canyons, coral reefs, and the cosmic wonder of solar eclipses.

Yet, it's throughout the changing seasons and monthly cycles experienced from the centuries-old cottage that is home to my husband and myself that most profoundly nurtures the way of the shaman within me. Here, my heart sings along with the quickening of tiny seeds in our garden, the hum of bees pollinating the growing plants, the vast and unceasing service of the microbiomes of the soils beneath our feet, and within my own body and engaging with the fifteen or more senses of the trees that grace our surroundings.

I soar with the sunset flights of swifts above our pond, wishing them well on their annual migrations in the Autumn and welcoming them back in the Spring. I revel in the diversity of a community that also includes the tiny shrews who've made a family home in the high grass at the edge of our lawn. And, thanks to my life-long communion with discarnate beings, I feel and am grateful for a joyous kinship here too, with Gaia's devic and elemental realms.

Our home became an even more appreciated sanctuary as we sheltered throughout the Covid19 pandemic. Physically constrained, the interweaving ways of sage, seer, and shaman guided me in the quietude to hear Gaia's voice more deeply than ever before. Continuing on from where *The Cosmic Hologram* completed, I was enabled to write a next book called *Gaia: Her-Story*.

It continues the narrative of *The Cosmic Hologram* to amass the scientific evidence of an in-formed and holographically manifested universe, vitally embodying an innate impulse to evolve from simplicity to complexity, diversity, and individuated self-awareness; to planets, plants, and people. Expanding the perception of life and living from biological organisms to the entire sentience of Gaia, her gaiasphere and the whole universe, it shows that everything in existence has inherent meaning and evolutionary purpose. Increasingly, the evidence it describes, demonstrates that evolutionary emergence isn't driven by random occurrences and mutations but through intelligently in-formational guidance and processes. In Gaia, its indomitable progress is embodied in planetary-wide collaborative and co-evolutionary relationships.

*

My life-journey has involved progressive entanglement and integration of the three ways of sage, seer, and shaman, and I greatly value how each can offer complementary perspectives that synergize into an embodied whole. Together, they've enabled me to perceive and be a participant in a co-creative, evolutionary, and fundamentally meaningful universe. And I've come to regard their paths as reflecting the many traditions that view such trinities as combining universal attributes of the divine masculine, feminine, and child.

For me, the way of the sage with its insightful understanding; that of the seer with its childlike wonder; and that of the shaman with its heart-based empathy, are all needed if we are to meet the challenges and possibilities of these transformational times.

When faced with personal and collective choices, and existential challenges, Gaia's example has breathed optimism within me. I'm invited, I feel, to embody a lived awareness that unity is our power, diversity is our strength, and love-in-action is our hope. It is with such unitive consciousness that we are to serve our communal opportunities to link up and lift up together, as co-creators and partners for Gaia and our ongoing conscious evolution.

*　*　*

Questions for Discussion

1. Jude noted "three main paths of discovery" on the spiritual journey: the sage, the seer, and the shaman. What is distinct about these paths and how do they relate to each other? Does one of them resonate with you more than the other?

2. Jude's explorations drew from "ancient and indigenous wisdom teachings of many traditions." To what extent has your path involved the exploration of ancient traditions? What wisdom do ancient or Indigenous traditions offer that we currently lack as a culture or society? Can you give some examples from different traditions?

3. Jude was also deeply invested in the wisdom of the sciences and what they suggest about the nature of reality. To what extent is your journey also informed by the sciences? What is the wisdom that science offers? In your estimation, does it complement or contradict spiritual sensibilities?

4. According to Jude, both ancient traditions and modern science "converge" on the notion of the "primacy of mind or

consciousness." Why is this convergence significant for the spiritual journey? What changes when mind is more fundamental than matter?

5. Spirituality is often seen in passive terms, but Jude came to realize that we exist to actively evolve and be co-creators with the mind of God. What does it mean for you to be a "co-creator" with God? What kind spiritual evolution are you undergoing now?

Sages to Explore

- Elisabet Sahtouris
- Isaac Newton
- Max Plank
- Erwin Schrödinger
- Albert Einstein
- Fred Hoyle
- Dennis Sciama
- David Bohm
- James Jeans

8: Unexpected Illumination

Karen Johnson with Hameed Ali (A.H. Almaas)

Hameed's route to inner discovery began in childhood. Deep, attuned care and nurturing from his mother, grandmother, and family environment provided a sense of safety that fostered the feeling that the universe is fundamentally a good place. This would prove to be a crucial element in his worldview and search for truth. It enabled him to journey into the unknown to face fears many individuals would find discouraging and insurmountable. Although he contracted polio before he was two, the illness did not cause a lifelong trauma. This is largely due to the underlying attitude that already had been established in him. Hameed survived the illness and thrived despite his physical disability. He walks with the aid of a crutch. This basic trust in the goodness of reality paved the way for the teaching that was to come through him.

In addition to that baked-into-his-bones confidence that reality is good, Hameed's inquisitive mind and sensitive nature created a fertile ground for study, knowledge, and directly felt experience. He claims that there was nothing particularly remarkable about him as a child that could predict what his life has become. He has, however, described moments that display a wisdom beyond his years. For instance, at twelve, he said to himself, *I will meet the world as it is and take in all it has to offer without rejection.*

Hameed arrived in the United States in 1962 to study physics at the University of California at Berkeley. At the time, the San Francisco Bay Area was abuzz with the human potential movement. It was a parade of spiritual teachings, vanguard teachers, and experimental therapies. Psychoactive drugs were also part of the rising interest in the consciousness exploration scene. Hameed ventured into this world first through Reichian breathwork and bioenergetics. Working with his historical material in this way that connected mind, emotions, and body helped clear the tension patterns of his body and sensitized him to more subtle experiences.

It was through the suggestion of his bioenergetics therapist that Hameed found his way to a spiritual group led by Claudio Naranjo. He joined Seekers After Truth (SAT), moved into a house with some group members, and spent the next three years engaged daily in the techniques and practices assigned to them. Naranjo invited spiritual teachers from many paths to the group, and Hameed had the opportunity to study with them in an intimate setting. Among learning many other forms of spiritual mappings and initiations, Hameed also studied the Enneagram with Naranjo, who had received that wisdom from Oscar Ichazo. The combination of deep psychological introspection and rigorous practices created quite a pressure cooker for the group. Hameed took it all on gladly. The new experiential knowledge that was burgeoning clarified his life intentions. He left his university studies just short of completing his PhD in physics as he began to recognize that the truth he sought was to be found elsewhere.

Even though spiritual experiences were plentiful for him at that time, Hameed considered them a dip in the ocean, and the shore was more commonly where he felt he stood at this point in his life. He thirsted for more than intermittent experiences, and wanted to understand them, rather than only enjoy their blessings.

His journal entries speak of longing, crushing heartbreak, remorse, openings, deep joy, and passionate love. For women, yes, which at his age was a pretty deep interest, but the main thrust was a desire to be one with

God and to be embraced by the Beloved, to be absorbed by the unnamed, finally content in union with his heart's desire.

It was during this time of yearning and devotion that the members of SAT were given instructions for a twenty-four-hour prayer. Hameed started his prayer day without question or expectation, with pure intention to follow instructions exactly. This is how he recounts the experience:

> In the practice I became aware of the internal functioning of mind and emotions, and I realized there was nothing I could do to change it. As I felt the objective helplessness of the ego consciousness along with a strong desire to be free of it, the helplessness resolved into completely giving up any attempt to change anything. It was a complete surrender that ushered in a strong, unexpected descent of a kind of blessing. I was bathed and showered with a full, syrupy, golden sweetness that tasted like pure honey. This began to dissolve the sense of body, and I heard the sound of buzzing bees filling the room until I finally lost consciousness. I don't know how long I was completely gone, but when I came to there was amazing clarity and awareness that made me feel "it was enlightenment." I went to sleep believing I was enlightened only to awake the next day in a pleasant place but not in that sense of enlightenment.

Although myriad cessations were yet to come, this one had a lasting effect. Hameed noticed that an experience of enlightenment did not signify the end of the path, and that recognition got him curious about how it happened, and when he would get snagged again. Nurtured by the blessings of this prayer, he practiced with even greater surrender, humility, and reverence.

As he encountered different teachings, Hameed approached every teacher's instructions with an earnest determination to squeeze every drop of learning he could out of the practices that were offered. This enabled many luminous openings, but feeling good or having spiritual experience was not enough. He wanted to understand his experience and how it came to be. He investigated himself and began to recognize the spiritual portals that correlated with the openings that the traditional techniques enabled. This cognitive detail did not derail him from his felt experience. Indeed, quite the opposite. As he gained speed on his teaching journey, this education would eventually benefit many others by helping to guide them to delve inward with great precision.

His explorations and discoveries continued for many years, long before it was clear to him that what was moving through would serve a purpose larger than his own personal desire for liberation. What all his experiences of unfolding had in common were love for the truth of whatever he was experiencing, and the wish to know and be himself fully and truly. Decades after his childhood resolve to take in everything without rejection, Hameed describes his experience after deep meditation:

> How lovely to be myself, to be content with what is—wanting nothing more, desiring nothing else. It's like magic, even greater than magic. The moment I say "yes" to my experience, with all my heart, regardless of what it is, the waves start to subside, the clouds begin to dissipate. Calmness, peace, gentleness, an exquisite contentment. There is no more cause for discontent, no more reason for holding or protecting. My body relaxes, tensions let go. My heart is so peaceful, so light, like the surface of a quiet and still lake. My chest feels as if it does not exist, as if the flesh and bones have evaporated. I feel a gentle breeze going through my body, touching the very essence of my heart. There are no more barriers. Oh, it feels so good. So fresh, so new. Joy comes in gentle waves, just as the breeze touches the petals of flowers. It wells up from unseen depths. It involves the entirety of me. How sweet my heart feels; full, overflowing with its own nectar.

> The breeze actually and literally blows within the cavity
> of my chest; the nectar is an actual soothing fluid that wells
> up, as if out of a spring right at the center of the chest. The
> experience is not physical, not emotional, not mental. It is all
> these together and more. When the heart opens, when the
> real nectar of divine love flows within the body, all boundaries dissolve, all categories vanish. I am a flowing nectar. I am a
> budding rose. I am intrinsic joy ...

He ends this journal entry with, "Such a unifying and vivifying experience of life is our rightful Inheritance as human beings. And it is only a glimpse, a flavor of the potentiality of human experience." He didn't yet realize that he was describing the specific characteristics of presence, which the Diamond Approach teaching revealed to him more explicitly years later. Along the way, some teachers took him aside to give him direct encouragement. They recognized something different about him. He never thought of himself as special or different and, in fact, that was one of his limitations. For a long time, he thought everyone was like him.

*

I met Hameed in 1970, just as he was beginning with the SAT group. One evening he showed up at my apartment to pick up my roommate for a meeting with Naranjo. There was a brief but notable moment between us as I was taken aback by the friendly gleam of his wide-open smile nearly expanding beyond his thin face. He peered into my eyes directly in a way that was simultaneously bashful. That was the first glimmer in the cascade of events that would unfurl a unique and undefinable relationship. It remains so to this day more than fifty years later.

From a very young age, my attention was drawn to unexplained perceptions and events. I saw energy fields around all living things, and sometimes inanimate things too. This became disconcerting to me when I realized it was unusual. My mother, although perplexed by it, didn't make me feel it was wrong. She simply didn't know why people had light around them.

My emotional history was more complex than Hameed's. I was bullied at school, and my parents parted ways when I was thirteen. Despite our many cultural and emotional differences, Hameed and I did have some formative elements in common. We both seemed to retain the sense that we were held in a loving and good way early on, which established in us an innate attitude that the universe was benevolent. And although neither of us were immune to pain and suffering, we shared an inner sense that somehow things would be okay no matter what happened.

Culturally, we couldn't have been more different. Hameed was brought up in Kuwait, which was a simple village in the 1940s, and I in post-war Palo Alto, where the whir of Silicon Valley was revving up. The Eichler subdivision of my neighborhood was unusually diverse for the time. Recently, I discovered that this was because Joseph Eichler would not go along with the redlining that other developers supported. It was a tight-knit neighborhood, and some of us who grew up there stay in touch to this day.

The freewheeling atmosphere of the Bay Area in the 1960s gave me delicious opportunities to explore myself and new realities. My mother and stepfather worked with me to heal some of my pain from the divorce and the social injuries I had experienced as a child in schoolyard encounters. They introduced me to yoga and self-hypnosis and happily shared what they were learning at Esalen. Given it was the 1960s, that was pretty rich!

I did regression work with my mother on hand to validate my perceptions of childhood experiences that I had forgotten. She was frequently flabbergasted at the level of detail with which I remembered things. They kept notes of my journeys as I spoke under trances. It was fascinating for me to see the secrets my psyche held.

My spiritual experiences were intermittent throughout my teenage years. A sense of peace or spaciousness or elation would arise as I chanted along with my Self Realization Fellowship records. All the consciousness exercises that I was learning didn't quench my thirst for meaning but served to whet my appetite for more.

One initial experience that had a lasting impact on me was brought about through medicine journeys. My first true boyfriend, who I had met in art school, escorted me on a peyote journey where I tasted and felt a pure, clear, soft, loving presence in my heart. Welling up and out, expanding all around my body and beyond, I perceived everything was a pure clarity and soft loveliness at once. My body was as light as a feather, and the sweetness was the most heavenly taste my mouth had ever known. It was as if my heart was tasting itself. In the Stanford University courtyard where we would hang out selling his flutes, I fell in love with everyone who passed by. I realized I was seeing the good in them and loving it, and then I realized they were made of this substance of love.

It turns out that the taste center that opened in my experience that day complements the discernment possible with the opening of the other subtle inner senses of texture (touch) and color (sight). We can know the qualities of presence—love, clarity, kindness, joy, strength, will and more—through the immediate perception of their color, flavor, and texture. The subtle realm of being weaves with embodied substantive presence to bring true fulfillment in the quest for meaning. The qualities of our nature are truths verifiable through the senses without being the usual worldly sensations.

The same year I met Hameed, I received shaktipat[1] from Swami Muktananda. Inching forward in a line waiting for the magic touch of the feather, I watched as one by one he touched a plume to each person's head ever so delicately. When my turn came, he put down the feather and swatted me on head. Humiliated, I walked away without much hope of fireworks or illumination. The next day, the sparkling shimmer of shakti rumbled awake, and then sputtered through me for weeks until my head popped with scintillating clarity and my heart began to spill love. The bubbling, clear aliveness is a force that continues to evolve for me.

---

[1] Shaktipat refers to the transmission or conferring of spiritual energy upon one person by another.

*

Around this time, Hameed received a transmission of a different kind from the 16th Karmapa, Rangjung Rigpe Dorje, during the Black Hat Ceremony.[2] Although many people reported expansion and light, Hameed immediately got a headache that lasted for a year. He visited all sorts of doctors. One Tantric practitioner told him it was gas. When Hameed finally had a chance to ask Tarthang Tulku what he thought was going on, the renowned teacher told him that there was light in his head. Hameed had no idea what the Rinpoche[3] meant.

It was during a period of meditation, after some time had passed, that Hameed felt something open in his forehead and begin to descend: a sensation of an unknown physical kind, an effect of palpably distinct hereness, certainly not an emotional feeling, a non-mental recognition of a substance. This was the moment that he recognized presence as the descent of a spiritual substance.

How was it that the Karma Kagyu transmission of clear light awakened for Hameed the luminous spiritual substance that is the source of the Diamond Approach? Years earlier, while still a graduate student in Berkeley, walking home from a restaurant one night, Hameed was hit by a motorcycle. The vehicle slammed into him as he stepped off the curb. He was flung into the air and looked down at his motionless body on the road. He was a clear, brilliant diamond consciousness. From this objective, transcendent yet located perspective, he peered into the world and saw both suffering and joy. Then gazing into another realm, he saw freedom and light. A choice was upon him. Move into the world or move into the luminous freedom? Love toward the world arose as a shimmer and drew him back to his body.

That night some kind of diamond consciousness was activated in Hameed. Although it operated throughout his subsequent studies,

---

[2] For over 300 years, Tibetan Buddhist monks, known as Karmapas, have donned the Black Hat in a ceremony designed to liberate participants from the cycle of birth, death and rebirth.
[3] Rinpoche is an honorific title for an incarnate lama or highly respected religious teacher in the Tibetan Buddhist tradition.

explorations, and discoveries, it wasn't until the transmission from the Karmapa that its function became more explicit. Hameed's experience of the Vajrayana empowerment didn't unfold how it usually does within that lineage because, in hindsight we can see that all the spiritual influences on his journey were fuel for his unique process, but he was not destined to continue in any existing lineage. Transmissions from other traditions were received without question but were sifted and integrated in specific ways that delivered particular understandings—this was the function of diamond consciousness. Hameed had no desire to control this process and simply noted the reality of how it seemed to be functioning.

The Black Hat Ceremony was only the beginning. It was such a profound experience that it would take time to completely develop in him. It seemed to bring up his ego content that was blocking the transmission through the usual resistances and defenses. Hameed set to work understanding the ego structures and unconscious material in his personality impeding the flow of his experience. The Karmapa's transmission transformed and developed Hameed by stimulating all the barriers and blockages to experiencing presence. It was at the end of that yearlong headache when Hameed experienced the descent of light from his forehead.

It took some time before Hameed recognized the full significance of the presence that was arising. The interaction with diamond consciousness, the true teacher for him, shifted his process from one of having spiritual experiences to one of being taught through inquiry and immersion about the logic of how presence was unfolding him and all of reality. He learned that presence is our true existence and authenticity. Hameed's limitless curiosity stimulated insight after insight to reveal the precision and clarity of the aspects of presence, which would lay bare the logic of the journey that had begun.

*

Hameed and I didn't cross paths again until 1972, when he and a friend decided to go to Boulder, Colorado to guide the Fischer-Hoffman process,[4] and I was invited to go along. As our tiny caravan of two cars made its way to our new home, he and I spent most of the ride together in my VW Bug. Although both of us were shy at the time, we were downright chatty the whole way. That day we started a conversation that has not yet ended. Our friendship grew in a nourishing sea of questioning and of enjoying discovery. The development of the friendship, the conversation, the inquiry, and the thrust of the teaching is all one and the same movement.

Hameed's allegiance always was to inner exploration, and nothing swayed him from that. It became clear that not everything that was happening for Hameed was understood by his teachers or friends. The SAT group had disbanded years earlier, and some of Hameed's experiences of presence were even discouraged by a teacher he had been studying with for a few years. After working for a while with the painful feeling of not being understood, he finally separated from that teacher when a solid gold diamond showed up in his chest at a meeting one evening. He was clear. Not in mind and heart alone, he knew as an embodied truth that he was headed in the right direction and needed to follow this presence to its utmost.

When he recognized the reality of this presence, and that it was reality within him, Hameed knew he had something to teach. Then he had the distinct realization that this presence was who he was. He was that medium itself in a nondual way, meaningful presence—which is the stuff of consciousness that knows itself—was the very beingness of what he also was. It was the nature and the core of his individual consciousness. He found himself again and even more deeply than before. This depth showed him that he was not only an individual whose nature is a purity of being, but also that this being is the being of everything.

Hameed was unfolding into new ways of knowing his inner nature and, at the same time, transforming from the conventional mode of

---

[4] The Fischer-Hoffman Process was an intensive psychotherapy designed to work with early childhood identifications. It has since developed into the Hoffman Process, a week-long residential retreat designed to help participants identify negative behaviors, moods, and thoughts that developed unconsciously during childhood.

being a person to being a true human informed by the inner being. Clear that he had discovered something true and rare, he then for the first time felt a resolve to teach it to others. He initiated a work group in Colorado and began using his inquisitive mind and heartful fervor to get to the real bottom of things!

I was part of that group but not fully, because I was straddling different roles. I was Hameed's friend, learning from him, and also learning with him. Our inquiries spanned all our waking life. In the grocery store, taking a walk, watching *Star Trek*, eating a meal, everything was game for discussion. The openness and joy of discovery between us was thrilling. Everything was new and fresh. We were having experiences we had never heard mentioned before, and we set out to find others who knew of such things. Our research did not reveal any exact matches.

Our form of inquiry would eventually be formalized as the central method of our work. The process of understanding as it is informed through presence is a revelatory movement fueled by the love of the truth for its own sake. We don't inquire to get anywhere or to move toward any idea of what we will find, but we simply immerse into where we are right now. It is love of the truth of our experience that rends the veils covering the truth of what we are. And the truth of what we are is not one truth or one state to attain, but all the ways true nature manifests. As an old Sufi saying puts it, "When I say this is true, I do not mean only this is true. I mean this, too, is true."

In 1978, I got married and moved to Denver with my husband, a young physician who was doing his residency at Denver General. Hameed had moved back to Berkeley in 1976, and then married Marie Bickford, a former fellow SAT member, in 1979. He would fly in from Berkeley every other week to do a three-day weekend group of teaching and practices.

We talked often on the phone, continuing our dialectic, and when he came to visit, we discussed and chatted and laughed and were quiet together too. Not trying to get anywhere, we went everywhere, into a marvelous new universe that opened our friendship. We discussed everything from relationships to what he made for dinner to the novel inner sense of how things were. There was such an open innocence to all and everything. Hameed's questions about inner experience and reality became more probing and pointed over time, challenging me in ways that brought forward issues to understand. The blockages were doorways to understanding the numinous nature of being. Stepping through them was not always easy, but I was learning more about my nature and reality. I had always wanted meaning, and it was appearing in ways I hadn't expected.

Hameed was excited about having discovered something wondrous, and he could see that it had not totally caught hold of me yet. One night as we sat in my living room in Denver, he asked me to reach out my hand. I did so without hesitation. He cupped his hand and circled it in the air, as though distilling and gathering something invisible. He leaned over and poured the substance into my open palm. I felt a viscous fluid filling my hand and saturating my flesh with shimmering substance.

The sensation got so strong! Its clear, awake fullness moved up my right arm and continued to flow throughout my torso, my heart and left arm, and then I felt it pooling in my belly.

I was gobsmacked as the radiant elixir traveled its pathway, enlivening my whole body with a sensation that can only be described as HERE I AM. My pelvis became a full, lucid density spilling down through my genitals, into my thighs, legs, and feet. I was lit up with its weightless mass.

It was the quintessence of hereness, the very substance of reality. I don't even know how I knew this. What I was feeling was presence— awakeness in its irreducible existence. Pure consciousness. "I see what you mean," was all I could muster. It was a divine fullness of being.

Our investigations of consciousness had until then opened to the lightness of being, but here now was the full recognition of substantial presence for what it was, in its purest form and value. This was new for me. The recognition of presence being what I AM was a next step, the sparkling immediate realization of the truth of self, albeit a no-self self. Realization in the Diamond Approach begins with this dazzling point, which is a point of departure into the boundless being of the nondual realms.

I was hooked by this presence, and it spun me in its radiance bringing out the best and the worst in me as my soul unraveled from the inside out. It had its own intelligence and timing. Painful stretching and falling into dark holes, ecstatic joy and peaceful contentment were all part of it. Then there were stages of stabilizing in being the realization I knew without doubt. Even so, that was a process that took many years. Our conversations deepened in tandem with our realizations, and over the years as our discoveries became more parallel, my ability to contribute grew.

This presence was ground zero for Hameed's groups. All the practices and meditations were for the purpose of the discovery and preservation of this human essence. In the beginning, Hameed taught without speaking explicitly of presence because he wanted to see whether the experiences we were having could be arrived at through inquiry. Was what we had discovered universal? Could others experience it too?

Hameed went about his investigation into this new phenomenon with scientific rigor. The presence we experienced in the beginning as a pure medium transformed itself over time into different qualities of being, each one beckoning specific regions of ego reactivity to be recognized, experienced, and understood. If his students explored and understood their ego reactions, would presence arise as it had for him? Could the results of inquiring into a certain issue be duplicated? Would anger open to red strength in the way we had experienced? Pain to the warm green presence of kindness? Would investigating the history of willfulness open to a true flexible will as support to be?

It turned out his hypothesis was a living one and was borne out again and again through inquiry into whatever was going on with someone. "Let's find out where you are and understand it totally," he would say. Just as it had been for us, it was through welcoming and meeting the low points, difficulties, and deficiencies that students opened more deeply to the riches of presence. Hameed guided students with surgical precision, probing into and beyond the limits of the known, and as he did so, presence would arise in a specific way to deal with the distortion of ego that was presenting itself. Soon his students were riding the waves of presence into the ocean of consciousness itself.

Working this way, the boundlessness of the great expanse emerged naturally. And not only one homogenous expanse of space, but there appeared different ways of experiencing the vastness of our nature: as love, pure presence, pure awareness, pure mystery, pure dynamism. Each way of knowing the nondual was a whole universe, and with each a new layer of ego would be shaved off and understood. Deeper and deeper structures evaporated as they were systematically understood, revealing the truth of our deepest innerness.

And that's nowhere near the end of the mystery of reality! Wonders never cease and our nature expresses itself in ways that defy all human categories, including those of dual and nondual. Space can loop and fold in and around itself, and we can know our nature beyond space and time as unilocal and unitemporal. We are not one thing as one state or presence or vastness. We are all things manifest and unmanifest, and all space and time and beyond at once.

Our understanding of the individual consciousness and the qualities of presence that emerge within it are unique to our teaching. Each one is a realization of the unfathomable truth of what we are as individuals, inseparable from the nondual, but truly nondual in the sense that the individual and the expanse are two ways of expressing one true nature, two sides of the same thing.

In our view, individual consciousness is true, meaning we do not consider it to be an illusion as some traditions posit. The vastness of being differentiates itself into precious organs of perception that are individuals of being. Beings give true nature eyes to see, hearts to have human relationships, legs to walk, fingers to touch, and mouths to eat. All our daily lives and all the spiritual realms we travel are experienced through our individual consciousness. The individual is a sensitive field of consciousness that is the perceiver and experiencer. We sometimes refer to this individual consciousness as the human soul. It is where and how all experience occurs.

The felt sense of individual consciousness is quite subtle, and we recognized it explicitly only after years of asking the question, "Who is experiencing this?" When we are feeling the vastness of the universe is what we are, even though there is no location of the individual, there still is local perception.

No matter the state—local, expansive, unilocal, or beyond—our individual consciousness is a lens through which the expanse can perceive the world and function in it. And it's also how we can know our full human continuum of experience. Being human is the openness to all experience of all realms and the ability to embody all of it. To be in the world and know our nature beyond it is to be a true human being.

*

After nearly a decade of witnessing many souls open to the palpable fullness of presence through the method of inquiry, it became clear to us that the natural unfolding logic of the process, the method, and approach was not simply a technique to open experience, but a bona fide spiritual path erupting into the world. The process of understanding that illuminated obscurations brought reality into view from so many surprising angles. Presence itself had written the directions and etched them into our soul. We had no choice but to surrender to its intelligent force that took us to the edges of itself, revealing its endless being.

History shows us that true spiritual paths are not invented. Most often they arrive unbidden as a force from beyond the familiar realms revealing themselves through unsuspecting individuals. Hameed was one such individual. He never has owned the teachings as his. He knows it is not possible for any person to create such an amazing display of knowledge. He was honed to read the messages that were etched into the souls of his students, his friends, and most importantly himself. He had the training of mind and body and the flame to pursue truth at any cost.

A teaching was born through the adventure of inquiry into his experience. As the captain of the inner space cruiser, Hameed discovered wisdoms not only for his own benefit but for the sake of any who are drawn to learn the truth of their nature. The experiential knowledge of this teaching illuminates universal human issues that correspond to the presences that can arise in different forms, qualities, and dimensions. He is clear that this teaching would not have unfolded as it has without the copilots and crew that were support and first-tier guinea pigs. And I am clear that the teaching found its spearhead and would have made its way through him in any case.

The Diamond Approach path to spiritual realization addresses the human needs of these times. Applied with love, sincerity, and steadfastness, open-ended inquiry is a diamond key. The inquisitive mind in harmony with the heart's love for the truth probes with kindness and discernment and enables our experiences to be understood. With precision and clarity, we can travel though ever deeper dimensions of the human soul along the continuum of experience from dual to nondual and beyond. Through the power of presence—the elixir of transformation—the human soul becomes the instrument that can live the subtle and the ordinary as one radiant truth in the world.

It doesn't make sense to say that Hameed and I found the divine or God or enlightenment. Something found us. We simply were lit up with the fire of love for the truth, which made us findable.

Fifty years after that ride in the VW Bug, our undefinable relationship continues to disclose new ways to know our nature. This living teaching develops and displays its wisdom jewels among the teachers, students, and practitioners of this path all over the world, hopefully rippling into the collective soul of humanity.

Over the years I can say I have earned my wings to fly by Hameed's side. The divine dialectic continues reaching new heights. I am honored to share this small but marvelous taste of our story with you.

* * *

Questions for Discussion

1. Both Hameed and Karen were nurtured by a "basic trust in the goodness of reality" and by an "innate attitude that the universe was benevolent." What does this mean to you? What would change in your daily life if you really grasped the goodness of being? If reality is benevolent, what then of malevolence?

2. Hameed's and Karen's journeys moved beyond the desire to just *have* "spiritual experience," to the desire to *understand* this experience. Discuss this distinction between experience and understanding in the spiritual journey. In what ways has your journey also consisted in a "process of understanding"?

3. Discuss what Karen and Hameed mean by "presence" in the spiritual path. What steps can you take to more fully embody presence in your own spiritual journey? Can you also identify clear "barriers and blockages to experiencing presence" in your life?

4. In speaking of Hameed's journey, Karen insisted that "spiritual paths are not invented" but rather "they arrive unbidden." Has this been true in your experience? What is the relationship between *invented* spiritual paths and *discovered* spiritual paths?

5. For Karen, it was not so much the case that "Hameed and I found the divine or God or enlightenment;" rather, "Something found us." What do you think Karen means by this? Is what you are seeking also seeking you? Why is this mutuality important in the spiritual journey?

Sages to Explore

- Claudio Naranjo
- Oscar Ichazo
- Swami Muktananda

- Rangjung Rigpe Dorjie (16ᵗʰ Karmapa)
- Tarthang Tulku

9: Finding God through Rivers, Dogs, and the Sky-Like Mind

Jay McDaniel

I had many mentors as a boy: loving parents, good friends, wise teachers. One of the most important was the Guadalupe River in the hill country of Texas. She—and I cannot help but think of her in gendered terms—is eighty-seven miles long and flows smoothly most of the time into the Gulf of Mexico. My parents would take me to the Guadalupe River when I was a child; and I was mentored by her color, her smell, and by the way she could hold you if you swam in her. You could never clutch her in your hands because she was made of liquid. But, like God, you could float in her and be supported.

Often, I would swim underneath her surface and look up at the world above, where my parents were having a picnic. Intuitively I realized that the world beneath the surface is as real in its way as the world above. It is a world of beauty, of silence, of darkness, and dreams. It is different from the surface world, but complementary to it. Often when I look into the eyes of people and animals, I see this river. All people have rivers inside of them. All people have depth dimensions, even if they do not know it. Our hearts always contain more than our minds can ever understand.

A friend jokes that the Guadalupe River made a Taoist of me. She (the river) helped me realize that life is flowing and fluid, and that the purpose of life is not to escape the fluidity, but rather to flow with it and in it, as best you can, and sometimes, if you are really lucky, to be absorbed into its silent beauty. It is from her underwater currents, and also floating on her surface, that I learned to "go with the flow."

But she may have made a Buddhist of me too. I am especially grateful to the Guadalupe River for helping me understand the wisdom of silence, because when you swim under her surface everything is so quiet. All you can do is listen and be amazed. All you can do is allow the preoccupations of your mind to fall away, so that you can listen to what Zen Buddhists call "the sound of one hand clapping," and then realize that in a deep way, that sound is everywhere—in the sheer activity of being alive—even in the surface world. Silence is not the absence of sound, it is the presence of listening; and the Guadalupe River helped me listen.

I was a churchgoer as a young child, and I still am. I know some Christians who might say that God "creates" rivers, as if God is one reality and rivers quite another. But I see things differently. I think God is a feeling, too; and that God can be found *in* rivers, just as God can be found *in* music, and *in* the eyes of other people, and *in* moments of kindness, and love, and play, and wonder. It was from our Lady of Guadalupe—much more than the words of the Bible—that I learned about mystery and beauty and silence, and about how you can swim in beauty without fully understanding it. When I wash my hands, I think of the waters of the Guadalupe. I think Jesus might have had an appreciation for rivers, too. He was baptized in one. Only after surfacing from the grace of the Jordan River did he realize his calling.

Transcendence

Does a river have a soul? I am not sure. Maybe not, if by "soul" we mean a particularized seat of awareness, a distinctive vantage point from which the world is seen. The Guadalupe River is more spread out, with many vantage points. And she is changing all the time. In this respect I think she illustrates the teachings of Buddhism. If souls exist, they are flowing and thus different at every moment. We never step in the same river twice, say the Buddhists, and even we ourselves are never the same stepper. The Guadalupe River is a vivid example of the liveliness of impermanence.

And yet certainly, amid her flow, she has *soul* in the African and African-American sense. Soul is depth and feeling, authenticity and beauty. She is filled with this kind of soul and thus immensely soulful. I think she would be much at home with the rhythm and blues, or the soulful explorations of Miles Davis' *Kind of Blue.*

Equally important, in her soulfulness, she has a welcoming spirit. She lets people swim in her; she lets children splash around in her; she lets people sit by her banks underneath the trees and have picnics, or read novels, or watch her currents.

Admittedly, sometimes she gets angry and shows a different kind of power. People have drowned in her. But she is generally a very safe and gracious river. A religion with much beauty—Islam—says that, in the last analysis, the mercy of the divine mystery takes precedence over the wrath. One time, when I was young, I saw the wrath of the Guadalupe River. She was overpowering. She was flooding, and she elicited in me a feeling of terrifying mystery, which is one way of feeling what scholars of religion call the holy. But I think her mercy is much more prominent than her terror. There is a teaching in Islam which says that the divine mystery has ninety-nine names, one of which is The Beautiful and another of which is The Merciful. I think these two names are the ways that the Guadalupe River reveals God.

She is also very independent, and in this respect, reminds me of the Hindu goddess Kali or, perhaps better, the goddess Ganga, whose presence is found in the Ganges River. I suspect that as a goddess the Guadalupe River is also a feminist. She does not *belong* to any of the people who swim in her. She is not male-defined; she is not dependent on the male gaze for her approval. She is her own person. Yes, some people might think they own her, or that they own rights to the banks by her; but really, in her beauty, she owns them. And that's the way they want it, deep down. Nobody really wants to own a river like the Guadalupe. Capitalism can't touch her. They just want to be close to her, and sometimes they confuse this with owning. If we use the language of "belonging," then she belongs to everybody but also to nobody. Here she elicits a sense of divine transcendence. Nobody owns God, either. Not even people who think they do.

Companions

I have said that God can be found in feelings. One such feeling is the sense of grace we humans receive from dogs, with their capacities for unconditional love. I say this because one of my companions in river absorption was a dog. She belonged to me and I belonged to her. There was a mutual belonging. She would swim above water most of the time, but she didn't mind diving into the depths. Her name was Patty.

Patty was like the Guadalupe River: beautiful, silent, mysterious, and flowing. Like all living beings, she was not simply a body; she was also a soul. Of course, she was not the only soul in the river. As I would swim underneath the waters, I would see the fish: perch, catfish, and minnows. They too were ensouled bodies. They also moved according to their own aims. There are so many kinds of soul, so many forms of beauty. Some are strange and scary: like the snakes, the water moccasins, who would swim in the Guadalupe River. But they are souls as well. Patty would bark at them and try to get close to them. I would try to swim away from them. Still, we were all swimming. This is part of what I mean by soul. I mean goal-directed feeling and activity that follows from it. When Patty would bark at the moccasins and yet get close to them, she was filled with goals. And when I would swim away, I was filled with goals, too. The fish would swim away from us, as would the snakes. They had goals as well.

But there's more to soulfulness than agency. There's also the capacity to feel the surrounding environment from a first-person or first-canine point of view. Or first-minnow or first-snake point of view, for that matter. To feel the presence of otherness, of what philosophers call alterity. In process philosophy this activity is called *concrescence*. It is the activity of subjectively prehending or feeling what is around you and gathering it into the unity of a single moment. Soul is not supernatural; it is ultra-natural. When we swim in rivers, when we look at dogs, when we see our parents having picnics, the rivers and dogs and people become part of us. Alfred North Whitehead says that the ultimate reality of the universe is the many becoming one in each moment of experience, whether human or canine. Every moment of our lives the many are becoming one in us and *as* us. That's a Zen idea: every moment in life is an incarnation of the whole universe. To see the universe in a grain of sand, said William Blake, is to see heaven. I see heaven in the eyes of a dog and the flow of a river.

Eachness

A little more about dogs. Many people like to talk in general terms about *all* animals and how we should respect *them*. This is noble language. Or if they want to narrow things down a bit, they may talk about the beauty of different kinds of animals, saying that we should protect endangered species. This too is noble. But in our rhapsodies about "allness" we can lose sight of eachness.

By eachness, I mean the singularity: the unique way that each animal presents itself to the world, staking its ground, and making its claim upon the world. Each human being is a node within the larger web of life but not reducible to any other node. And so it is with each animal. Each animal is a subject, endowed with capacities for feeling, intelligence, memory, anticipation, perception, and aims.

This subjectivity is the animal's eachness. In order to approach the eachness of an animal or, for that matter, another human being, it can help to have a sense for rivers.

There is an old Zen story that speaks to how we might "know" a dog. A monk asked Zen Master Joshu if a dog has the Buddha-Nature and

Joshu answered "Mu," which literally means *not*. This confused the monk, because he knew, as did Joshu, that all living beings have the Buddha-Nature, dogs much included. But Joshu's Mu was a wise saying. He was inviting the monk to let go of all speculative questions concerning animals and the Buddha-Nature, and simply "be" in the present moment. This is the heart of Zen. It is to experience the sacrament of each present moment, whatever the moment happens to be, and to respond with wisdom, compassion, and freedom, as best one can. The Zen way is very river-like. It is free to adjust to each new situation.

I remember years ago riding in a car with a friend of mine from Japan who was a Zen priest and who, later, became a Zen master. I was his English teacher for one year while he was studying in the United States. We saw a dog crossing a lawn just to one side of the car, with a bone in his mouth, strolling toward a place where he would hide it. My friend—the late Keido Fukushima of Kyoto, Japan—turned to me quickly and said: "Jay, do you see that dog?" I said "Yes." He said: "That dog is a Zen master." That made sense to me. Every living being is a Zen Master. Some people just don't know it.

Newness

A young friend of mine once asked if dogs go to heaven. His dog had died. I said that they did. He was glad to hear it, and then added, if they happened to go to the other place, he'd want to go there too. "Who would want to go to a place without dogs, without rivers, without other forms of life?" A friend of his had said dogs don't have souls. I said I disagreed with his friend, and that sometimes I thought maybe dogs are so beautiful that they have many souls, maybe even more than people have. He and I agreed that dogs are pretty special.

How many souls does an individual dog have? It is hard to say. Our human souls change with each and every experience. Who we are at age thirty-six is different from who we were at twenty-six, which is different from who we were at sixteen, which is different from who we were at six. Imagine the crest of a wave as it moves toward the shore. The crest is different at every moment, carrying with it a past that accumulates more memory over time. This cumulative past is like karma.

But the present is always more than the past, and it is in the present that freedom lies. We can use the phrase "individual soul" to name the wave as a whole (from its beginning until it reaches the shore), or we can use the phrase to name each moment of the crest. If we use it in the latter sense, then we are a series of souls—a series of concrescing moments—which inherit from their predecessors with a certain kind of intimacy. The same situation obtains with a dog. Every time a dog barks she is a slightly new dog. A slightly new soul.

For my part, I feel grateful to the Guadalupe River for teaching me about dogs, and I feel grateful to Patty for teaching me about the Guadalupe River. There's so much beauty to be seen in our world, even in its sadness and tragedy and horror. So much wonder. So much eachness.

Some people think the beginning of wisdom lies in a fear of the Lord. But surely it can also begin with delight in beauty. The Lord finds us through the waters of a river in whom we float, the eyes of a dog who swims along with us, and in the wise teachers, the loving family, the good friends, who can mentor us into abundant life, moment by moment.

I'm a Christian myself, and it's because I believe in sacraments. I think Jesus was a sacrament whose own openness to life, and especially to the poor and powerless of the world, was an invitation for us to appreciate sacraments wherever we find them: in the wisdom of Zen priests, in the wisdom of dog priests, in the wisdom of river priests.

The Clearing

I don't sharply distinguish sacraments from priests. A priest is someone who helps you become more open to God. And a sacrament is something that does the same. For Christians Jesus is a priest who walked the hills of Galilee, and also a sacrament in the bread and wine of the eucharist. He shifts shapes, like water.

I think God, too, shifts shapes. God is found in the soul of a dog and in the fluidity of rivers, in the eyes of a friend and in the depths of an ocean. I think God reaches out to people, and into people, with the images they need in the moment at hand. Process philosophers call them "initial aims," but such language is a bit too pedantic for most people. Just call them callings or fresh possibilities or energetic lures.

Does God stay the same amid the callings? Is there someone or something behind what calls? I think so, but like a river, or another human being, or a lake, or a dog, it is wide and deep. The best I can say at this stage of my life is that God feels like a Clearing, an Open Space, a Sky-like mind. Here's how I put it my book, *Living from the Center*:

> [T]his creative and moment-by-moment universe unfolds within the larger context of an infinite Clearing—an Open Space—that is everywhere at once. This infinite Clearing is the mystery at the heart of the universe...this Open Space is not an empty vacuum that adds nothing to the universe, but rather a sky-like Mind filled with Wisdom, Compassion and Freedom.[1]

Even today, I think the center is a clearing and the clearing is a center. I try to live from the center as best I can, sometimes successfully and often failing, trusting that its wisdom, compassion, and freedom embrace me and all, with a love unearned, yet graciously revealed through all our teachers, all our mentors, rivers and dogs so much included.

You

I realize that words like "clearing" and "open space" can suggest something real and beautiful, but also impersonal. Most of us do not think of open spaces as persons. In *I and Thou* Martin Buber reminds us of

---

[1] Jay McDaniel, *Living from the Center: Spirituality in an Age of Consumerism* (St. Louis, MO: Chalice Press, 2000), 154.

the dangers of living in a world where everything is an object and not a subject. A relationship between I and It, he says, is very different from a relationship between I and Thou. In closing I want to say something about thou-ness or, as I will put it from now on, about you-ness.

I'm sure it's clear to you that for me dogs and other animals are subjects of their own lives and not just objects for others. And the same applies in a very special way to other people. No person is an It; each person is a You. The philosopher Emmanuel Levinas gives us the beautiful phrase: "the face of the other" and suggests that our moral lives begin, not with abstract principles and ideas, but with encounters with the other person or, as I would add, the other animal, the other river. All living beings—and all beings are alive in some way—are in their own ways a *you* whom we encounter. Native peoples speak of the various creatures in the universe as all our relatives. This makes sense to me. We are all part of a single family. As I see things, the clearing in which our lives unfold, the open space, is likewise a You. The clearing is a You in whose heart all yous live and move have their being.

One evening many years ago I was driving down the highway with my oldest son, who was about eight years old at the time, and we found ourselves awestruck by the incredibly beautiful sight of a night sky with its thousand points of light. I'd been reading a book which told the story of a famous British actress Lillah McCarthy, who was a friend of the playwright George Bernard Shaw. At one point in her life, she was deserted by her husband and went to Shaw for advice. She cried and cried in his presence, and once the crying stopped, he asked her to walk outside with him. They walked for a while in silence. Then Shaw said to her: "Lillah, look up at the sky. There's more, there's so much more." What she saw in that moment was a gorgeous display of stars in the sky, and she was reminded of the fact that they (the stars) had lives of their own and that her own life, including even her suffering, was not the center of things. She found it consoling that she was not the center, and I do too.

With this story in mind, I asked my young son what he felt when he gazed into the sky. He thought for a second and then said: "I don't know

Dad. I guess I feel *small but included.*" His phrase *small but included* struck me like a lightning bolt. It helped me name something I'd been feeling for a long time, namely that the whole universe, and we ourselves as creatures among creatures in a small but gorgeous planet, are some-how included in a larger whole that is much more than us, but somehow friendly to us: a sacred whole. I know that some people have a sense for this sacred whole, this inclusive context, but do not think of it as having a life of its own. The sacred whole is, for them, the sum of its parts, pure and simple. But it does not feel that way to me. It feels more like a mind, a self, a life, a consciousness. When I speak of the sky-like Mind above, I think of a You not an It: a reality to *whom* we can reach out in prayer.

I think I know the reason for this. As a young child, when I was about eight, I was sitting in the backyard with my mother on a quiet night underneath a dark and starlit sky. I had been taking confirmation classes at my church, seeking to understand the faith into which I was entering, and I had questions about Jesus. I asked my mother who Jesus was, and she offered an answer I've never forgotten. She said: "He is someone who is always holding your hand, even when you don't know it; and holding the hand of everything else, too."

This was the biggest idea I had ever encountered at the time, and it is big for me still. It is the idea that there is a loving Companion who is holding the hand of everyone and everything all the time: all the animals, the mountains, the rivers, and, of course, all the people. Not just all but *each*. As a Jewish friend puts it, the loving Companion cares about us and knows our names.

It was only years later, when I was introduced to the philosophy of Alfred North Whitehead, that I could render this idea into terms that made philosophical sense. Whitehead spoke of this side of God as "the consequent nature of God" and viewed it as that side of the divine which feels the feelings of all living beings, all the time, with, in his words, "a tender care that nothing be lost." I think that's what my mother was talking about that night. She was saying that Jesus is a name for that side of God which is, again in Whitehead's words, a "fellow sufferer who understands." If you lean in a Buddhist direction, you might think of this side of God as a cosmic Bodhisattva, a goddess of tears who weeps with each and all: Kuan-Yin.

I think of this Bodhisattva, this Companion, every time I look into the sky. My name for her is God. I don't think I ever thought of God as all-powerful. All beckoning, yes. All inviting, yes. All loving, yes. But thanks to my mother and her understanding of Jesus, God was never, for me, a bully in the sky overly preoccupied with rules of conduct. God was and is an eternal Companion to the world's joys and sufferings, and an inwardly felt lure toward the fullness of life for each and all. It is almost as if Kuan Yin emptied out a hole in her very heart, so that we might have a space to roam. Just as a loving mother is made complete by the joy of her children, so God is completed by the joys of the universe.

I also feel called by this Companion. The call doesn't come in words but in feelings, and it is inside me. Sometimes it is a whisper and occasionally a shout. It is a call to love, to be honest, help others, to realize I am not the center of things, but also to realize my potential. It's also a call to be curious, delight in surprise, and help build a better world where no one is left behind. A call to sustainability, justice, compassionate community.

Every morning when I get up, I walk onto the front porch and gaze into the sky. Usually it is early, before daylight. I say to the sky: "In life, in death, I give myself to You." I mean a little something like what Jesus said when he surrendered his spirit to his Abba. I offer my prayer because, after all, every day is a living and a dying, and every day is a gift. What is important is to surrender our spirits to the open space, to the clearing, to the companion, to the love, however we might name it, each day; and then move forward in the day, as best we can, adding goodness and beauty to the world, as best we can. No need for perfection. It is important to be forgiving, including of ourselves. But no need for despondence either. Always we can be sensitive to the presence of something wonderful, full of life, not only in the vastness of the totality but in every creature. In dogs, rivers, people, in life. All are included in a something more that can be addressed as You, that beckons us into love, and that holds our hands, with tender care, even if we don't know it.

Yes, the unity of the universe is a divine You and we are always within this You. The You is within us as our better self but also beyond us as a sky-like Mind that includes us all. Moment by moment, day by day, we can all express a little gratitude for being alive. We can all say, in whatever language makes sense to us: I give myself to You.

*   *   *

Questions for Discussion

1. For Jay, mentors are not just human, but can also be geographic and canine. What non-human mentors have contributed to your own spiritual journey? Can you point to a certain landscape, river, or pet that has added to your path? What do you think you've added to them?

2. Jay said that "God can be found in feelings." What does he mean by this? Can you point to moments in your life when you have *felt* God? What were these feelings like? For Jay, it's not just the case that you feel God, but God also feels you? From God's perspective what do you feel like?

3. Jay made a distinction between the "supernatural" and the "ultra-natural" when speaking about the many-souled world. Why is this distinction important? What changes if we view God as ultra-natural rather than supernatural?

4. Jay's journey led him to become aware of the sacramental nature of the spiritual life. What does this mean? What is a value of sacraments to the spiritual path? Can you also be a sacrament?

5. Consider whether your default relationship to the world is an "I-It" or an "I-Thou" relationship. What is the difference between these? What changes when the world is revealed to be

not a conglomeration of objects, but a community of subjects? Is God an object or subject?

Sages to Explore

- The Guadalupe River
- Miles Davis
- Alfred North Whitehead
- William Blake

- Keido Fukushima
- Martin Buber
- Emmanuel Levinas
- George Bernard Shaw

10: *A Journey of Integration of Science and Spirituality*

Amit Goswami

My journey began with spirituality. Some of my earliest and happiest memories are of inspired moments in the company of my father who was a Brahmin guru in India at a very small scale.

My first lesson in physics is a good example of what I later started to call "happy" physics, physics that makes you happy. I was maybe six years old and was taking my first train journey. Don't be surprised; this is growing up in small time British India in the early 1940s. The journey was in the very least intriguing. I remember leaving the station in the evening. I kept up for a while, then succumbed to sleep. In the morning, I woke up and found that we were at a new station. *Amazing*, I thought. Then my elder brother asked, "So, did you enjoy it?" I hesitated, then said, "Yes."

"How come there are two kinds of train?" I asked. Everybody seemed to be surprised by the question. "Yes," I said, "one kind that moves by you fast, and the other kind, the one we are in, just seems to shake except in the beginning. Still, it has brought us to another station." Then everybody started laughing, and I was embarrassed. They were obviously laughing at me, at what I said.

"But why?" Somebody took kindly to me and told me about physics and the relativity of movement. We cannot tell from a moving vehicle of constant speed if it is moving, or everything else is moving by. So, for another train passing by we see that one moving; but for our own train we can tell the shaking movement, but not the constant speed of ongoing movement. If we look outside, however, we will see the trees moving by; and of course, we'd think, trees don't move, and figure out that it is we who are moving because the train is moving. And now that it was daylight, when the train started moving again, I verified what he said, and I was happy.

Why was I happy? In retrospect, I think because I saw that physics is not abstract. It is useful for living our lives. It matters.

Later, when I had my PhD, moved to America, and got a tenured position at a university, it was different. Physics was instrumental for all this. Exploring physics satisfied my ambition, but I was more and more unhappy. I was unhappy with my life, and physics did not give a clue about how to restore happiness to it. And vice versa. My life had no bearing to the physics I did for so many hours of my day. *What a schizophrenic living*, I could not help thinking.

My collaborators at the University of California at Berkeley and I figured out a new application of quantum mathematics to atomic nuclei and plotted the result in some striking looking figures—or so I thought. But when I came home and my wife asked me, "How was your day?" I showed her the pictures. I had them in my briefcase. She said, "What are they?" I proudly said, "Well, that's how nucleons—nuclear inhabitants—move about in nuclei that are called deformed. Aren't the pictures beautiful?" My wife promptly said, "You are out of your mind." And my balloon busted.

In 1973, I was invited to an American Physical Society meeting to give a talk which was considered quite prestigious. I gave my spill which I felt went quite well, but the feeling did not last long. As other speakers presented, I felt they were doing a much better job and naturally getting more attention, and I was jealous. The jealousy only increased during the course of the day. In the evening, I went to a party in honor of the speakers and now I was getting jealous because others, not this handsome dude—*moi*—were getting more attention from the females at the party. At 1 a.m., I noticed I'd exhausted an entire packet of antacids, and still had heartburn. I felt disgusted and went outside. The party was being held at a place called Asilomar on the Monterey Bay. As I stood on the terrace, the ocean air hit my face and a thought came out of nowhere: *Why do I live this way?* At that very moment I knew: I don't have to live this schizophrenia between my life and how I make my livelihood. I can integrate. I can do happy physics. I can become whole again. This was my discovery of the archetype of wholeness which I continue to pursue. Archetypes—wholeness, love, and beauty for example—are the noblest contexts of our thoughts.

Later, when I was researching creativity, I found that this kind of breakthrough is called a crystallization experience: when you discover the archetype that you're destined to follow. The formation of a crystal from a solution is a bit of a mystery. The experiences crystallize similarly in a mysterious way when something that was potential in you becomes actual. Reincarnation theory tells us that this potentiality called *dharma* is a choice we make before taking this birth, and we bring suitable propensities from past lives to fulfill our dharma.

Here is the important thing: dharma really is about spiritual values—what religions call "virtues" and Plato, "forms." Objects such as Truth, Love, Wholeness, Abundance, Power, Justice, Goodness, Beauty, and Self.

I have observed that this theory is true. Before this experience, I was an ordinary and mediocre scientist. I excelled in my field of nuclear physics, but that was because nuclear physics no longer attracted *crème de la crème*. And yet after my wholeness experience, not immediately afterwards, but with some work, something changed. It is as if there were abilities in waiting that now were reclaimed and I could do things that I never thought I would be able to do—among them solving the quantum measurement problem, integrating science and spirituality, developing a quantum science of feelings and emotions, integrating alternative and conventional medicine, integrating all the different forces of psychology, developing a scientific theory of reincarnation, developing a scientific theory of life and its evolution, answering questions that molecular biology and Neo-Darwinism cannot address, and even developing a new paradigm for capitalism. And all these outer accomplishments pale in comparison to the transformation that took place in my character, like the capacity to love. Not instantly, mind you; it took many years, but it happened.

So, let me say, this is the key to quantum living: Pay attention to meaning first; sooner or later this will lead you to purpose and archetypes. And when you pay attention to them, they reciprocate and the crystallization experience or an archetypal dream will tell you about your dharma. The other thing of significance that happens as you pay attention to intuition and archetypes is that you discover there are feelings in the body that accompany the intuitions—a feeling in the gut or an expansion in the heart. You discover also that feelings are more reliable than your thoughts; they don't lie.

In this way, when purpose has entered your life, life becomes meaningful, juicy with vitality and satisfying with creative pursuits and accomplishments. You've gained access to subtler forms of happiness and this is not a zero-sum game. Once you find the archetype of your choice, my suggestion is: Do some outer explorations with it first. In other words, engage with it using outer creativity, with the objective of making an outer representation of it. This is where traditional professions help us begin the archetypal work, and this is why we need what I call quantum activism to straighten out the professions so they can become archetypal once again.

It is a shame on our academic culture that when I turned to investigate Truth using science, and made the greatest discovery of my life, the entire physics profession had gone helter skelter. Hardly any working physicist recognized the value of what I did, although retired physicists did so by quite impressive numbers. I had to find my professional supporters elsewhere, in the fields of medicine and psychology, personal growth and spirituality. Even business people were more receptive than physicists.

Only recently did I have enough courage to pursue Truth in my inner life. I did better with Wholeness. As I was exploring Wholeness with outer creativity in the fields of science and spirituality, medicine and psychology, I was also finding a balance between creativity and conditioning, inner (dreaming) and outer (waking), and male and female in me using inner creativity. The inner work is far from finished of course.

What about Love? Love to me has been more or less an inner exploration. When love confirmed what I discovered about unity as a creative insightful thought, the knowledge acquired became wisdom to live life in a new way. Once I found love, my heart opened, and that helped my outer explorations in all aspects of life as well.

The story told in this essay roughly spans the period 1973 to 2018, the most melodramatic period of my life. Read the story told in the upcoming sections as the story of an unfolding. Many of us begin like a contracted consciousness of a flower bud, but there is the potentiality of becoming full-bloom. And then one day the bud begins to unfold. That's my story.

Meditate, Meditate, Meditate

There is a story about a tourist visiting New York. He is looking for the way to Carnegie Hall. He sees a passer-by who seemed reliable, so he asks, "How do you get to Carnegie Hall? The passer-by is a musical maestro. He replies, "Practice, practice, practice." Indeed, if you want to perform at Carnegie Hall, the maestro's advice is good. But what good is it for the tourist?

What happened to me is similar. I was looking for not one, but two Carnegie halls. One was the answer to the question, "How do I integrate physics with living my life?" The second was, "How do I learn to love my wife?" The people who I thought were reliable would all answer, "Meditate, meditate, meditate." But meditation, from what I knew about it, was the way to God, spiritual enlightenment. Do I have to be enlightened to find answers to my questions?

The Bible says, "Whoso knoweth love, knoweth God." The reverse could be true: whoso knoweth God, knoweth love.

In the West, God usually means an almighty individual, often pictured as a white male with a long beard; as the king of kings, God stands as a model for the mortal king's majesty and authority. Some are scornful about this gendered depiction, but would it be any different if God was a white female? The great Indian poet Kalidasa was a devotee of the female goddess Saraswati and he wrote a salutation to her. But you know what? The salutation glorifies the twin peaks of the goddess more than anything else. That is not particularly spiritual, is it?

I am being facetious. In the East, where I grew up, there is no scope for making this confusing picture of God. In the eastern traditions, what they glorify is a Oneness or Wholeness. Reality is not this, they say; the world of multiple objects is illusion for which the Sanskrit word is *maya*. The gods (spelled with a small "g") like Saraswati were archetypes whose exploration helps get you to unity; that is their only importance.

I of course rejected the concept of Oneness as God long ago because it made no scientific sense to me. How are we one, when every part of the being I know dwells in separateness from you, even when you are my intimate one?

Could I find eastern guidance to God or Oneness in America? Since the 1960s, eastern spirituality has been gaining popularity in America. The Hare Krishna movement, for example. The Beatles popularized Maharishi Mahesh Yogi and his transcendental meditation (TM) movement; the philosopher Alan Watts and Zen master Suzuki Roshi popularized Zen Buddhism; Swami Muktananda brought the idea of Shaktipat or kundalini energy. Jiddu Krishnamurti was another popular name on the scene, and there was Bhagwan Shri Rajneesh who later became

Osho. Other Hindu teachings go back even longer: Vivekananda and his Vedanta societies, Paramahansa Yogananda established a group, too, the Divine Life Society, on so on.

Even in Eugene, where I lived, I could find Zen and Tibetan Buddhism, and a Muktananda group. But wherever I went, the advice was common: "Meditate, meditate, meditate." So, one day, I did.

Who Am I?

I never tried TM because I had already tried guru-given mantras and concentrated on them when I was in my teens in India. Nothing much happened. Of course, you could say I was simply not serious then, which is true. When I went back to spirituality, the first group that attracted me was a Muktananda group. Swami Muktananda was a new age celebrity for giving "*shaktipat*" to people—a jolt of energy that feels wonderful. I never felt moved to have shaktipat, but I chanted with the Muktananda group a lot and meditated with them too. Again, nothing much to report. After a couple of years of all this, I decided to go back to my family practice, a mantra recitation called *japa*. This time something happened. This was fall, 1976.

Japa is a simple repetition of a one syllable mantra in your mind. After you do it for a while, the mantra is internalized. What that means is the mantra goes on inside you somehow even when you are attending to other chores. So, it was supposed to be going on while I taught or when I read a scientific paper. Once in a while, I'd check this out, and it was true. Whenever I checked, the mantra was right there. After I did this for seven whole days, as I said, something happened. It was so special that I wrote it down the experience:

> On a sunny November morning, I was sitting quietly in my
> chair in my office doing japa. This was the seventh day since I
> had started, and I still had a lot of energy left. About an hour
> of japa, and I got an urge to take a walk outside. I continued

my mantra deliberately as I walked out of my office, then out
of the building, across the street, and onto the grassy meadow.
And then the universe opened up to me.

> ... when meadow, grove and stream
> The earth, and every common sight,
> To me did seem
> Appareled in celestial light,
> The glory and freshness of a dream.[1]

I seemed to be one with the cosmos, the grass, the trees,
the sky. Sensations were present, in fact, intensified beyond
belief. But these sensations were pale in significance compared to the feeling of love that followed, a love that engulfed
everything in my consciousness—until I lost comprehension
of the process. This was *ananda*, bliss.

There was a moment or two of which I don't have any
description, no thoughts, not even feeling. Afterwards, it was
just bliss. It was still bliss as I walked back to my office. It
was bliss when I talked to our cantankerous secretary, but she
was beautiful in the bliss, and I loved her. It was bliss when I
taught my large freshman class; the noise in the back rows,
even the back-row kid who threw a paper airplane was bliss.
It was bliss when I came home and my wife hugged me and I
knew I loved her. It was bliss when we made love later.

It was all bliss.

The feeling of all bliss did not stay long. By the end of the second day, it
started fading. When I woke the next morning, it was all gone.

A comparison with the literature told me that what I experienced
was called *sananda samadhi*, samadhi with bliss as an aftereffect. The

---

[1] Wordsworth, "Ode on Intimations of Immortality from Recollections of Early Childhood."

Sanskrit word samadhi stands for a convergence of the two poles of experience, subject and object. In our ordinary ego experience, the split of subject and object is huge and quite distinct. In my experience, in that split second, there was hardly a distinction.

Who am I then? The more stable ego-I, or this very special oneness—the I that took seven days of meditation to precipitate? How can the brain produce both experiences? Also, the aftermath of the experience—bliss—came to me as a capacity to love anyone. I was curious. Can one have this capacity to love not just temporarily, but permanently? So many questions and no answers. *Is this how it's going to be, my journey of integration?* I could not help thinking.

I did entertain the idea that this oneness experience might be what mystics call enlightenment, out of which comes transformation. There was unconditional love for two days, but as I said it faded away. So, no permanent transformation of the brain had happened. Perhaps my experience was a glimpse at what transformation is like? Then how could transformation elude me for long?

How to Interpret Quantum Physics

When the aftereffect of my "big" oneness experience faded away, I was disappointed that nothing came out of it. In retrospect though, something did. I found my happy physics: the quantum measurement problem. Quantum objects are waves of possibility, with the capacity of being at different possible positions. When we measure, though, we find the object in one position as a particle. How does the wave become a particle? The mathematician John von Neumann had proven mathematically that material interactions could not "collapse" a possibility wave (many positions) into the actuality of a particle (one position). What then, does? Von Neumann proposed: the observer does; his consciousness chooses the actual position out of the many possible positions to affect the collapse. But this, too, is a paradox for a couple reasons:

1. Consciousness is supposedly a brain phenomenon. What else can it be when everything is made of matter—what all physicists including me believed at the time? But that contradicts von Neumann's theorem, right?

2. There is the alternative called dualism: consciousness and matter are separate realities. But here, too, a paradox: Suppose you and your friend simultaneously measure a quantum object. You choose one outcome, but he chooses another one. Whose choice counts? There is no science to discern that!

Then, in 1982, the world of physics was shaken up by the Aspect experiment showing that if two photons (quantum objects of light) are "correlated" by interacting up-close, they become entangled and capable of communicating instantly even at vast distances. The two photons become one. There is that oneness again. Do quantum objects of possibility reside in a domain of Oneness? That domain must be outside of space and time, where separateness prevails, where you need signals to communicate, signals taking time going through space.

In 1985, most scientists subscribed to an interpretation called the "many worlds interpretation." In its simplest form it says that as a measurement occurs, the world divides into infinite worlds. In each of the worlds is manifest each of the facets of a possibility wave that has yet to collapse. Yet, the multiple worlds by definition cannot communicate. So how do we ever verify such a theory? Without verification, an idea is not science.

I had a feeling, an intuition that von Neumann was on the right track. On the side of my conviction was an interpretation of quantum physics given by Werner Heisenberg himself, *the* Heisenberg who, along with Erwin Schrodinger, discovered quantum mathematics. Heisenberg said what we call collapse is a change in our knowledge about a quantum object. Think of that old thought experiment: an electron spread all over a room with a roomful of Geiger counters. Before measurement and collapse, we know only possibilities and probabilities about the object's position; after, we know exactly where the object is. Etymologically, the word "consciousness" comes from two root Latin words, *cum* and *scire*. *Cum* means "with" and *scire* is a verb that means "to know." Consciousness is the vehicle *to know with*.

When von Neumann tried to take Heisenberg's idea further, to consider the actual measurement situation, with his thinking that the observer's consciousness chooses actuality from possibility, he encountered the paradox of the two friends measuring the same event simultaneously. Whose choice counts? So close, yet so far—or so I thought.

I was not an optimist in those days. But it was spring, and my friend Frederica had invited my wife and I to her house in Ventura, California to spend a week. I met Frederica at Esalen; we had a romantic moment that formed a lifelong bond and though we both transcended romance, we became friends, or more appropriately, Platonic lovers. So we went, and Frederica's energy was catching. I was happy again.

So, this day in May 1985, we went to hear the great mystic Jiddu Krishnamurthi (JK) who was speaking at nearby Ojai. This was the first time I heard JK. He was over ninety, then. His hands trembled a little because of Parkinson's, but his mind was sharp. As usual, he was chastising his audience about present centeredness, radical awareness, as in his books.

One guy was heckling him: "Radical awareness does not come to us sir, what to do?" And Krishnamurthi looked at him with his big, kind eyes. He said gravely, with great dignity, "It must come." Krishnamurthi's "it" was the "presence" of which he spoke often, which is enlightenment. The way he said the words inspired me beyond belief.

That evening, Frederica had invited a friend of my wife and I at our request, a friend named Joel Morwood. Joel was a Hollywood filmmaker; but he heard the siren song and went on a quest and was enlightened; he told us his experience which was utterly believable. So, I respected and liked Joel. But that evening we got into an argument, Joel and I. This one lead to the most consequential experience of my life, so I kept notes from which I quote:

> Joel and I got into a conversation about Reality, and I was giving him an earful of my ideas about consciousness, arrived at from quantum theory, in terms of the theory of quantum measurement. Joel listened with attention. "So, what's next?" he asked.
>
> "Well, I am not sure I understand how consciousness is manifest in the brain," I said, confessing my struggle with the idea that somehow consciousness must be an epiphenomenon of brain processes. "I think I understand consciousness, but..."
>
> "Can consciousness be understood?" Joel interrupted me.
>
> "It certainly can. I told you about how our conscious observation, consciousness, collapses the quantum wave...," I was ready to repeat the whole story.
>
> But Joel stopped me. "So is the brain of the observer prior to consciousness, or is consciousness prior to the brain?"
>
> I saw a trap in his question. "I am talking about consciousness as the subject of our experiences."
>
> "Consciousness is prior to experiences. It is without an object and without a subject."
>
> Joel was making his trap wider. But I am the physicist. I have answers better than him. He is just a filmmaker. So I said not a little smugly, "Sure, that's vintage mysticism, but in my language you are talking about some nonlocal aspect of consciousness."
>
> But Joel was not distracted by my terminology. Now he was visibly angry with my sophistry. "You're wearing scientific blinders that keep you from understanding. Underneath,

you have a belief that consciousness can be understood by science, that consciousness emerges in the brain, that it is an epiphenomenon. Comprehend what mystics are saying: Consciousness is prior and unconditioned. It is all there is. There is nothing but God." The last sentence he practically shouted at me.

That last sentence did something to me that is impossible to describe in language. The best I can say is that it caused an abrupt flip of perspective—as if a veil lifted. Here was the answer I was looking for and yet had known all along: *Consciousness is the ground of all being—and matter, including the brain, are quantum possibilities of consciousness that are chosen.* And sure: One can do science with this basic metaphysics. I was sure of it.

You may have read about the paradox of Plato's cave. A cave dweller is strapped in a chair so he can only see a shadow show projected on the wall in front of him. The shadows are representations of real objects that Plato called archetypes or "forms." The cave dweller has to make an about turn to see the real archetype instead of the representations, the shadow show created by the projector. All my academic life, I have been looking at the archetype of Truth as projected by materialist scientists. When Joel shouted at me, I made an about turn, I looked directly at Truth and saw it.

If you familiarize yourself with the spiritual history of the world, you will find that my story is not unique. Hui Neng, the sixth patriarch of Chan Buddhism in China (from which Japanese Zen originated) is supposed to have been enlightened when he heard something similar to "There is nothing but God" in a marketplace.

I have just used the word enlightenment, above. Am I claiming that I was enlightened by this discovery of mine? Perhaps I could; I know people who have. But why should I? To me, enlightenment is not about how to think, but about how to live. Enlightenment requires transformation.

Of course, right thinking helps right living and eventually I did turn my mind to "quantum living." But I am a scientist and the archetype of Truth was one of my preoccupations. So, my initial attention went to right thinking, how to think Truthfully.

Later that evening when everybody had gone to sleep and I was alone, I went outside. The Ventura air was hazy and the night sky was hardly visible, but in my imagination the sky became the radiant one of my childhood, and suddenly I could see the Milky Way. In my childhood, I was told that the Milky Way is the boundary between heaven and earth. Now I knew better, but no matter. I knew the difference of heaven and earth now, the scientific difference, I thought. In heaven, in the domain of potentiality, encompassing potential objects and potential subjects, there is only oneness marked by nonlocal signals of communication. In the domain of actuality—space and time—communication requires signals, takes time, and separateness is compulsory.

The kingdom of God is everywhere, said Jesus. "But people do not see it," he lamented. "They do not see it because you mystics never explained it properly," I muttered to Jesus. "When you say *everywhere*, you mean everywhere in heaven—the domain of potentiality."

No mystic ever spelled this out and the result has been confusion lasting millennia. Now, with the concept of a possibility wave and the domain of potentiality scientifically sanctioned by the Aspect's experiment, it finally makes sense to pedantic, practical people like me. I included these and many other insights in my book, *The Self-Aware Universe*, which at last earned me some high-level attention. One day, the psychologist Stan Grof called me and praised my book. Then the president of the Institute of Noetic Sciences (IONS), Willis Harman, invited me to write a monograph for IONS on my current research.

Meeting with the Dalai Lama

I joined IONS as a senior research fellow with the sponsorship of the Infinity Foundation in 1998. In the same year I met Brother Wayne

Teasdale, a great Christian spiritual man at a Theosophy get-together. Wayne and I resonated. He had already read my book and said it was of great help to him for the book that he was writing, *The Mystic Heart*. So, I was not surprised when, later that year, I received an invitation from him to join a mostly American group of scientists to visit H.H. the Dalai Lama in Dharamsala, India. The idea was to present a progress report of all the new paradigm research that I and the other scientists were doing. We would be conversing with one another and then there would be direct interaction of this group of thirty with the Dalai Lama. Another larger group of sixty would watch the interaction from an outer circle, but did not participate.

Sounds great, right? Unfortunately, while the group of five to which I belonged was discussing what to present of the quantum worldview when our turn came, discordance broke out unexpectedly. I had taken the lead and perhaps a little grandiosely was presenting the idea of how the way I interpret quantum nonlocality as the unity consciousness mystics talk about was the only way. Science was now supporting the spiritual metaphysics like that of Tibetan Buddhism without equivocation. But I got interrupted; my friend, physicist Fred Alan Wolf, took exception.

"Amit, you are assuming. You go too far. Not all of us new paradigmers feel we need to go that far."

"But in view of Aspect's experiment, quantum nonlocality is not debatable and that means in the domain of potentiality that possibility waves reside such that everything is instantly interconnected. This is oneness. Couple it with the observer effect; you identify oneness as consciousness, the ground of all being. Now bring in the brain in how quantum measurement takes place. And you get a theory of how the brain gets its self and how consciousness gets its subject-object split."

I thought I explained my whole theory quite well in just a few sentences. But Fred didn't agree. "You should read about the transactional interpretation."

I interrupted. "I know it. It makes ad hoc unverifiable assumptions..."

Fred interrupted back, "As if we can verify that consciousness is the ground of all being?"

I was getting upset. This was not supposed to happen. Fred wrote the foreword to *The Self-Aware Universe*. He was supposed to be in my corner. I said something in retort, and Fred said something in retort, and sooner than I knew, a fight broke out and even others joined in.

The organizers became concerned and complained to the Dalai Lama, who said something like, "Scientists will be scientists." Then he laughed and laughed. That did it. That—and his presence. Soon Fred and I and the others too were saying friendly things and all was okay.

Or was it? There was much time lost with all these shenanigans going on. So, the organizers made each of us present their individual work in two minutes or so.

I went first, but what could I say in two minutes about a solution to the quantum measurement problem that took me years to solve and more years to write about? The Dalai Lama listened but did not comment. I ended up very disappointed.

The next session though was very valuable to me. The Dalai Lama challenged us scientists to apply our models to the solution of social problems. That I took to heart.

The rest of the week was spent with watching dharma combat—how monks debate—drinking yak butter tea, and some of us making understandable, but mushy and inane comments. At the end, the Dalai Lama gave us all an important initiation.

All this was being filmed on video and was made into a documentary called, *Dalai Lama Renaissance*, by film-maker Kashyar Darvich. I found out about that a few months later when at a conference someone said, "I saw you in a documentary. You are very different as an actual person from how you are represented in the film." I sheepishly admitted: "I have not seen the movie. But I must confess that I did engage in a stupid altercation with another physicist. So what you saw is also real me."

But I was also a little curious. So when the filmmaker wrote to me a few months later and told me that he was coming to Eugene to show the film, we met and watched the film together. Even today, I advise people who take my workshops on transformation to see this documentary to get some idea of what transformation does to your energy.

Quantum Activism

Tackling health and healing with the new science gave me confidence. So when the president of the World Business Academy called to invite me to become a fellow of that academy, I was surprised and readily accepted. I took it as an event of Jungian synchronicity.

The president wanted me to write an article on how the quantum worldview affected business and economics. Soon I had a wonderful idea of extending Adam Smith's capitalism by adding Abraham Maslow's hierarchy of needs. When their survival needs are met, consumers turn to satisfy their higher needs which to me meant feeling, meaning, and purposive archetypal values. And if the need is there, gifted people—producers—always respond to demand. I wrote up my idea and the World Business Academy published it in three parts in their bulletin. *Not bad for a physicist to accomplish!* I thought.

At the time, Hampton Roads was publishing my work on the scientific evidence for the existence of God in a book called, *God Is not Dead*. Originally, I intended the book to have a section on social applications of the new paradigm. But the evidence itself already made enough material. I had to find a title for a new book to publish the rest, and the idea of *quantum activism* came to me while I was talking with my publisher Bob Friedman.

What is quantum activism? Through my personal journey, I saw that the integration of thinking, living, and how we make our livelihood are the three key ingredients of personal growth. Like all activists, quantum activists also work on social change, but they do it within the context of their own personal growth. The combination of these is quantum activism.

I wrote the book and named it, *Scientific Evidence for God Is Already Here, So What Are You Doing About It?* Quite catchy, I thought; but my editor had a different idea. He took the advice of his marketing people and named the book, *How Quantum Activism Could Save Civilization.*

Soon after publication, a woman named Renee Slade called to invite me to give a weekend workshop on Quantum Activism at a place called Yachats on the Oregon coast. I gladly accepted, although it involved frantic travel from Honolulu (where my friend Dr. Paul Drouin had started Quantum University on the internet with the ideas of this Quantum Doctor as the pivot). But I made it, the workshop went well, and Renee's friend Ri Stuart even videotaped the lectures.

A few months later, the two women showed up in my office at the university. "What's up?" I inquired after the usual pleasantries were exchanged.

"I am bored," said Ri. I didn't get it. Seeing me bewildered, she explained, "After your workshop, all Renee and I talk about is your movement of quantum activism. We want to be quantum activists. And I have decided to make a documentary about you and your work and call it *The Quantum Activist.*"

Wow! Then I remembered, Ri was this hot shot computer person who made $600 an hour for her services. She was bored of that because it was often more routine than could satisfy her creative mind. Ri continued: "We both looked at some of the footage of your workshop that we made and it looks pretty good quality. If we film you some more and put all those in perspective with additional footage from the internet and old movies, I think we can do it, make a pretty good documentary."

"A sequel of *What the Bleep*, huh?" I joked.

"We could if we had any money to hire an actress like Marley Matlin. But we don't have enough money. With what we do have, I think we can produce a pretty good documentary. But we need you. What do you say?"

"I say yes. Let's do it."

So began two years of filming. Mostly they filmed me talking about my work at various places of the university campus, but once or twice they filmed me in my office. Then the director of the Institute of Theoretical Science, where I had an office, got wind of this. I have no idea if that had anything to do with what happened next. Ri and Renee thought it must have; it was too much of a coincidence. The director literally kicked me out of my office. He visited and gave me two days to vacate.

In a panic, I called Ri and Renee at once and the two women found me an office, called the movers, and shifted my office within the apportioned time. We established a business: Center for Quantum Activism. A sign with that name appeared on my office door. It was official. Naturally, Ri created a website in my name but the objective was to publicize quantum activism and the center for quantum activism. She also created a website for their movie. That movie, *The Quantum Activist*, was released in 2009 in Seattle. We all went and the event was successful. We had a full house in a small theater, but the attendees were enthusiastic.

Ri was submitting the movie in various film festivals in the documentary category. It did manage to win a few awards. Then the big break came when PBS in Berkeley invited me to present the movie while they telecast it. I must have done a pretty good job, because twenty-two affiliated PBS stations ended up showing the movie and my interview.

My publisher in Brazil, Adriano, who was already arranging quantum activism workshops for me in Sao Paulo, got the movie subtitled in Portuguese. It was a great success in Brazil. Finally, even I made some money from it.

In the following years, the Quantum Activism movement started gaining traction in Brazil, United States, Europe, and eventually even in today's very materialist India. In 2018, my fellow activists and I established Quantum Activism Vishwalayam, an institution of transformative education. Vishwalayam is a Sanskrit word meaning "Home of the World." Today we teach over forty students from twelve countries pursuing their masters and PhD in quantum science of health, prosperity, and happiness. My hope is that our students will arrive at some transformation and become emissaries of how the integration of science and spirituality allowed by quantum physics can transform humanity back to civilization once again.

Wholeness and Quantum Spirituality

I will end with a few more words about my 1976 samadhi experience of the archetype of wholeness. The archetype of wholeness is an aspect of conscious Oneness, and many teachers think it is Oneness itself. I think not. The archetype of self, upon examination turns out to be no-self and leads you directly, when you experience it in samadhi, to the state of unconscious Oneness where you merge into oneness. You do not exist anymore as a separate self. You are liberated from Samsara.

This was not so with the wholeness archetype, in my experience, however. It is more like other creative experiences; you manifest the product of your samadhi experience and you do it by transformation—integrating all the dichotomies that create conflict within you.

The physician Valentina Onisor and I have recently written a book called *Quantum Spirituality*. This book is based in living life in the exploration of wholeness, staying in Samsara, and serving the world. This is quantum activism based in quantum spirituality. I see it as a never-ending journey consisting of integrating dichotomies and conflicts like living and livelihood, and especially the head and the heart. This has been central to my journey and my own activist spirituality. It's not easy, but I tell you it is worth it. I've found that I get to live in expanded consciousness much of the time. I invite you with all my heart to share this space with me.

*   *   *

Questions for Discussion

1. At the heart of Amit's journey is the wholistic integration of his living and livelihood as a physicist. Consider the relationship

between your life and livelihood. Are they separate and at odds? What steps can you take to integrate them in a more wholistic way? Why is this spiritually important?

2. Amit offered important advice for the spiritual journey: "Pay attention to meaning first; sooner or later this will lead you to purpose and archetypes." How do you understand this statement? How are meaning, purpose, and archetypes like Wholeness, Oneness, Beauty, and Truth related? Consider whether or not you have been pursuing a particular archetype in your spiritual journey.

3. After identifying the "archetype of your choice," Amit encourages "outer explorations" or representations through creativity. Consider the ways in which creativity is a mode of expressing the depths of archetypal reality. What "outer explorations" are you engaging in? What is the place of creativity in your own spiritual journey?

4. Through attention to intuition and archetypes, Amit discovered that "feelings are more reliable than your thoughts; they don't lie." What do you think he means by this? Can you give some examples from your own journey?

5. Amit drew a direct connection between "quantum activism" and "quantum spirituality." What is—or should be—the relationship between spirituality and activism? In what ways can spirituality support activism and activism support spirituality?

Sages to Explore

- Ramana Maharshi
- Alan Watts
- Suzuki Roshi
- Swami Muktananda
- Jiddu Krishnamurti
- Bhagwan Shri Rajneesh (Osh)
- Swami Vivekananda
- Paramahansa Yogananda
- John Von Neumann

- Werner Heisenberg
- Erwin Schrödinger
- Hui Neng
- Fred Alan Wolf

- Wayne Teasdale
- Stanislav Grof
- Abraham Maslow

11: Soul of the Cosmos

Becca Tarnas

My journey towards knowledge of the Divine began on a small farm. This might perhaps be surprising from the perspective of where I am today, a practicing archetypal astrologer and a professor of imagination and psyche. Yet my path toward an ensouled cosmos started when I first placed my hands into the soil of the Earth, saw the gift of life spring forth in the growth of edible plants, and came to understand the true meaning of a good day's work.

At the age of eighteen, situated at the significant threshold between high school and college, I chose to spend my summer working as an apprentice on a biodynamic farm located in the Round Valley of northern California. For the previous thirteen years I had been educated at a Waldorf School, thus the opportunity to practice Rudolf Steiner's biodynamic agriculture was a natural outgrowth of my education. That summer changed me utterly; I had been a bookworm who lived in her imagination, and my relationship to the natural world was one of reverence and awe, an intuitive perception of enchantment for which I did not yet have the right language. But learning how to work with the Earth to coax forth nourishment and sustenance, to tend ongoing relationships of care with horses, cows, sheep, and chickens, and to discover my body's resilience and capacity to work with diligence and devotion, gave me a connection to the embodied world that I lacked.

We would start our work days on the farm before sunrise, the promise of dawn tinging the horizon, the colors of a vibrant rose, mists clinging to the fields and twisting about the root of the distant trees, until finally the Sun's rays chased the moisture away until evening. The Sun dominated our days, scorching heat baking our skin and feeding the plants its nourishing light. After dusk the stars would come out twinkling into a sky undisturbed by light pollution, constellations and planets telling a story I did not yet have the ears to here. But night after night I would gaze at those stars, and feel myself held within a sacred cosmic womb that I had few words to describe.

Working thirteen hours a day, five and a half days a week, sometimes in 116° weather, showed me the true cost of good, healthful food. My values began to shift, and I devoted myself to learning about balanced ecosystems, human nutrition, and the encroaching threat of climate change and the ecological crisis. Live Power Farm was so named because the power of the farm is supplied only by living bodies, the horses pulling the plow, cows and other animals providing manure for compost, human beings doing the mental and physical labor, and sunlight powering panels and plants alike.

Prior to my time at Live Power, I thought that when I went to college I'd major in English literature and theater arts. Although my passion for theater and literature remained, when I reluctantly left the farm at the end of the summer and started my undergraduate degree at Mount Holyoke College, I chose to go in a different direction of learning. I committed to be an environmental studies major instead.

Four years taught me a great deal about ecosystems, habitats, and biology, about environmental collapse, global warming, and food injustice. I even learned of the importance of poetry and storytelling for cultivating a relationship with the natural world. And while this education was immensely valuable, I always felt something important was missing—a larger narrative that made sense not only of the particular details of the ecological crisis but also answered the question of how we ended up in a crisis to begin with. What were the cultural conditions that allowed modern humans to be so disconnected from the Earth that we could bring our ecosystems to the brink of destruction? What I didn't yet realize I was missing was the context of *world view*: What kind of a world view led to such disconnection and destruction, and what were other world views humans lived within that were more connected, holistic, and ensouled?

The answer, to my utmost surprise, arrived when my father came out to the East Coast to give a lecture to a group of Jungian psychologists in Vermont, and I naively asked if I might sit in and listen. I should share at this time that my father, Richard Tarnas, is a cultural historian and archetypal astrologer, and has published two major books on these subjects: *The Passion of the Western Mind* is a narrative history of Western culture and civilization, beginning in ancient Greece and culminating with the postmodern era, while demonstrating how history unfolds in death-rebirth cycles that mirror the gestation and perinatal process of a human infant. And *Cosmos and Psyche: Intimations of a New World View* presents considerable evidence of significant archetypal correlations between the cycles of history and the positions of the planets relative to one another. This controversial body of evidence demonstrates that the ancient practice of astrology, far from being disproven and irrelevant as the modern paradigm would insist, can shed extraordinary light upon collective history and the human psyche.

I entered the lecture room in Vermont only having a cursory understanding of my father's work: up until this time I paid little attention to it, knowing only that he was a professor of cultural history and depth psychology, and understanding that astrology had something to do with it all. Sitting shyly among an audience in which most members were twice or three times my age, I was utterly captivated by my father's lecture. He spoke about the modern world view, and how the modern human sees himself (the masculine gender used not entirely arbitrarily in this context) as a distinctly autonomous individual, separate from his fellow human beings, as well as from nature and the cosmos. The modern human self is a center of meaning, purpose, and intelligence, while the surrounding world is devoid of soul and consciousness. In contrast, my father also spoke about a primal world view, lived by our ancestors and by many Indigenous cultures still living today, in which the self is porous to the natural world, and meaning, purpose, and intelligence saturate the individual and the cosmos alike. Both self and world are ensouled from the perspective of this world view.

As I sat listening to this lecture, I realized that the answers I'd been seeking in all my environmental studies classes were being spoken right here by my own father: the separative world view of the modern mind had created the context for the great ecological catastrophe that was beginning to unravel disastrously all around us. In a state of surprised awe, I recognized that the path I thought I had been following out into the world, was actually leading me home again to my place of origin. I knew then I needed to study my father's work.

Although this is the story of my own spiritual journey, it is deeply entwined with my family lineage as well. This awakening to what had been at home all along brought me into the field of research with which my father had been engaged since the early 1970s. While working on his doctorate on psychedelic psychotherapy, he went to the Esalen Institute, located on the California coastline of Big Sur, to study with Stanislav Grof, the pioneering Czech researcher whose work focused on the healing potential of LSD psychotherapy, holotropic breathwork, and other non-ordinary states of consciousness.

In Stan and my father's work together, they searched for a method to predict the quality of experience an individual would have with a psychedelic medicine. There is great variability to psychedelic experience, and an individual taking a substance on one day might have a radically different experience several weeks or months later with the same substance, even if the environment, parameters, and dosage were all exactly the same. Likewise, two individuals taking the same substance at the same time, in the same dosage and setting, could have completely differ-ent experiences. One individual might enter the eternal contractions of a hell-state, while the other would be floating in the womb-like bliss of an oceanic paradise. The full range of standard psychological tests could not solve the mystery of this experiential variability.

However, one day a seminarian named Arne Trettevik, who was in one of Stan's workshops at Esalen, asked if Stan and my father had looked into transit astrology. With their western academic backgrounds, my father and Stan were both fairly skeptical of astrology; nonetheless, they were open-minded enough at least to look into the subject, since all other approaches to the problem of psychedelic variability had come to naught. Transit astrology tracks the movements of the planets through the solar system, making note of specific geometrical angles that planets make to each other, and then interprets these placements based on the archetypal meanings astrologers have come to recognize are correlated with the planetary bodies. After learning the basics for calculating astro-logical birth charts and planetary transits from Trettevik, my father and Stan compared the detailed notes from their own and others' psychedelic sessions with the corresponding transits and were amazed to discover that the symbolic meanings astrologers associate with the planets accu-rately reflected the nature and quality of their sessions.

I had known peripherally about this research as I was growing up, especially as Stan Grof was a godfather figure in my life, and as a young person I had the privilege of meeting other significant figures in the fields of both psychedelic research and professional astrology. But it was not until listening to my father's lecture in Vermont that I realized the ques-tions I'd been asking about the state of the world had answers within his work and in the writings and teachings of other individuals I had already met. I began to read my father's books and sit in on his courses at the California Institute of Integral Studies. I started to study the basic techniques of astrology, learning the archetypal meanings of the plan-ets, qualities of the geometrical aspects, the complex configuration of the zodiac, and timing of planetary transits. Simultaneously, I began independently to explore what psychedelics had to teach me.

The first psychedelic session I underwent was so beautiful yet simple, and in retrospect felt like the building of trust between myself and my psyche. Sitting on a rock facing the ocean, I began to set foot into a new realm, a different way of being. *Am I feeling everything? Or nothing? I am flashing between feeling nothing and seeing patterns in everything. Spiraling bubbles flow forth on the stream forming Neptune's forked trident. The moss is greener than anyone could imagine. There are infinite swirls and spirals in the white foam of each crashing ocean wave. Every rock, movement of water, cloud or pattern in the sky is engraved with deep, intentional patterns of beauty.*

When I closed my eyes for the first time it was as though I'd opened them to a deep, inner world. The first time I did this I saw all color, oranges and yellows forming skull-like shapes, some of them fleetingly familiar. Then, the image before me turned into a butterfly.

Every time I closed my eyes, I saw butterflies. Wings of every shape and size, layering and unfolding onto each other. The visions were magenta, orange, and yellow, with accents of vermillion, red, violet. I began to gather the images around me, building a warm, thick cocoon of butterflies around me. The sounds outside the cocoon grew softer. As I pulled all this energy into myself, I began to take new form, my body shifting into the shape of a butterfly. Even the colors of my clothes were melting into my wings.

I could feel, rather than see, the Sun setting behind the rocks that jutted out into the ocean from the cove. Just at the moment before it disappeared the glowing white-gold orb changed into the shape of a butterfly, hovered before me, then came directly into my heart. At that moment, I heard someone say, "Where did the Sun go?" and I could feel the answer: "Into me."

When a caterpillar enters its cocoon and begins metamorphosis its body dissolves entirely; everything that the caterpillar once was is gone.

The transformation is guided by several sets of embryonic cells that provide the only continuity between the caterpillar and what it will become once it emerges from its cocoon. These powerful cells have an apt name: imaginal cells. Within the rich culture dissolved in the chrysalis the imaginal cells grow to form wings, legs, antennae—a new body entirely. As the author Richard Bach writes, "What the caterpillar calls the End of the World, the Master calls a Butterfly." The bridge between death and new life, it seems, is the imagination.

The experience of transmuting into a butterfly established my connection with these sacred medicines that had the power to bring one into a molten mystical state. Such medicines are a central component of my spiritual practice and psychological growth, and while I recognize their extraordinary value for healing and transformation, I also acknowledge that such powerful substances are perilous and can lead into dangerous territory if not used responsibly. Working within a lineage that holds a sacred cultural context for such medicinal work, and seeking out the support and care of trained guides, are elements I see as essential for respectfully and consciously engaging with psychedelic medicines and non-ordinary states of consciousness.

My most pivotal experience with sacred medicines in terms of my relationship with the Divine took place less than one year after I had seriously embarked upon this exploration of astrology and psychedelics. Seated in an exquisite multistoried temple, while listening to the strange music of bells and gongs, voices composed of wisps of spirit began descending, spiraling into me, communicating through words, whispers, images, music.

These voices told me the reason I had become a butterfly on the beach in my first session was so that I could come to this place to learn my mythic name—what at the time I took to be my true name—*Psyche*, whose oldest meaning is "butterfly" in Greek. The name was bestowed at this time to allow me to see my connection to the whole, the butterfly as one small creature carried by the breath of the world, one fragment participating in, honoring, and in awe of the Soul that encompasses all things.

Following waves of extraordinary revelations about my personal life, it was then that I encountered the archetypes. As I closed my eyes and gazed upward toward the heavens, I could feel that all the planets were so excited that I was finally listening to them that they were each telling me who they were all at once. It was far too much to take in, and I asked them please to come one at a time. One by one, but first the Sun and the Moon, each planet introduced itself, revealing how its multidimensional and multivalent appearances in the incarnated realm were really all unified into single archetypes in the transcendent realm. With each planet I encountered qualities I had learned before in my study of astrology, and yet other qualities which were new to me:

The Sun, radiant presence, gold, singularity of vision, shone through me, through everything; nothing else existed in that light.

The Moon, cradling and being cradled, softness, a silver sheen of lavender comfort, holding in warmth, fullness, and settled contentment.

Mercury, a quickening pace as my thoughts raced to catch up, a rapid quill spelling, articulating, word, glance, taste, touch, sound, senses singing.

Venus, a verdant green of flowering beauty, vines growing in curls that turn into exquisite art, the silver sparkling of dew under leaves, mirroring a reciprocity of love and heart-warming presence, the shiver of pleasure and desire.

Mars, a flaming red heat burning through me with energy, action, anger, force, violence, blood, rushing in a hiss of fiery passion.

Jupiter, uplifting to a panoramic sweep of glory and triumph, images of great civilizations flourishing in their crowning moments, a spiraling climb to the grand arches of the Kingdom of Heaven, laughing, just laughing, releasing into giggles, soft joy, lips kissed by a smile.

The smile faded into a serious fixed gaze as Saturn entered my field, making me sit straighter, feeling the structural strength of my bones, my skeleton, holding me erect and steady, the stability of age-old institutions weathering through time, weathered away by time—time who eats his children—feeling my body slowly decay in death, yet somehow feeling reassured by this dying that comes again and again in repetition, knowing that all things must come to an end, and with that final acceptance at last can come wisdom.

Lightning-quick Uranus burst through, not settling into a single color or image, always overturning, breaking out, breaking through, a pace impossible to follow as sparks of creative genius flew off of every new idea to explode in firecrackers opening up ever unexplored future horizons.

All dissolved, and no sense of myself remained as the oceanic oneness of Neptune washed over all that had come before, containing everything in its synchronous holism, a peaceful oblivion of floating in a flowing celestial realm of watery image, ethereal spirit, and imaginal soul, transcending all boundaries.

With a rending tear, the ocean ripped apart into a volcanic chasm. Pluto gaped open swallowing all in titanic destruction, a violence so deep it was beyond fear—rather a pulsing of life impulse to survive or perish, pushed and pressured by the unbounded force of desire, fangs, torn flesh, rotting corpses, pushing through the excrement, massive desolation laying waste, decomposing, turning over, evolving through pain, passing through the white hot burning fire and from the dead ashes reborn. Then white light. All the colors melted together, every image unified. Only light.

After all the planets had introduced themselves, I asked if there was anyone else who wished to speak. In that moment the *Anima Mundi* made herself present. I felt deeply reverent, a tiny butterfly bowing down in awe, and yet she also indicated to me that I was her, we were one and the same. It was the most humbling, yet also empowering moment of my life. I began to get a glimpse of how the unity of the Anima Mundi refracts into many yet also remains whole, becoming the archetypes, which incarnate through the planets, which in turn incarnate in humanity, as well as in every fiber of the cosmos. It was like seeing how white light passes through a prism, and comes through in a dazzling rainbow of color, with each archetype as its own color, yet with no limit to how many colors could be present.

After this mystical encounter, I could no longer see the world without perceiving the archetypes living through everything. It was as though my sight had changed, and where before I would see a lovely flower, or a beautiful landscape, or a dazzling sunset, now I also saw the archetype of Venus, or the Platonic eternal form of Beauty, radiating through each of these particular manifestations. In athletes I saw Mars; in maternal care I saw the Moon; in technology I saw Uranus; in riches I saw Jupiter; in language I saw Mercury; and in time and tradition I saw Saturn. I could not go back to not seeing the archetypes everywhere. Not only did I perceive these archetypes in the human world, they shone through in the natural world as well: Neptune in the waters, Pluto in the fecund cycles of birth, procreation, and death; Saturn in gravity and bones, Venus in the ordered beauty of the cosmos. This change in vision was so encompassing, I now saw these archetypal principles as a pantheon of Gods. At the time, it was easy to feel like I had discovered the objective truth of the Divine, the true nature of God—or the Gods. But that perception was to go through a humbling period of integration as I encountered the field of participatory spirituality within the discipline of transpersonal psychology.

Participatory spirituality, especially as articulated by the scholar Jorge Ferrer, is a conception of the Divine as an indeterminate spiritual Mystery with which human cultures and individuals participate to enact the diversity of religious traditions, spiritual paths, and mystical encounters that we have seen flourish around the globe throughout history. Rather than espousing the perennialist philosophy of an objective spiritual truth to which different religions and spiritual traditions have varying degrees of access and understanding, participatory spirituality sees each religion or spiritual encounter as a co-creative event enacted between the human individual or specific culture and the indeterminate spiritual Mystery. Rather than an objective truth being discovered, a spiritual reality is elicited or called forth in co-creative relationship. Such a perspective affirms the diversity of religious and mystical experiences without creating a hierarchy of religions and spiritual traditions.

As I wrestled with bringing my own mystical encounter with the planetary principles into the context of a co-creative and enactive participatory spirituality, I began to recognize that while my vision of the particular planetary archetypes might not be the ultimate spiritual truth above all others—meaning Mars was not more real a God than Yahweh, or Neptune more primary than Krishna—the archetypal patterning itself might nonetheless be an essential quality of the spiritual Mystery no matter what form in which it was enacted. While Jorge Ferrer posits that the indeterminate spiritual Mystery cannot be described by any particular positive attribute, such as dual or nondual, personal or impersonal, I wondered if the attribute *archetypal* might actually be complex, diverse, flexible, and encompassing enough to describe the nature of the Divine without in any way limiting the multiplicity and multivalence of its expressions. Archetypes, as recognized by Jung, exist *in potentia*, and they are not constrained by their countless manifestations, but express forth ever anew in each subsequent age and paradigm. The archetypal perspective, rather than being an independent spiritual path, can be a complement to other religious traditions that can demonstrate which archetypal principles are most valued or carried by that lineage.

Philosophers since antiquity have engaged with the theory of archetypes, trying to understand whether they are transcendent or immanent, autonomous or participatory, abstractive or ontological, psychological or spiritual. Even as these discussions from over the millennia diverge and disagree with one another, it has been clear there is some underlying patterning to the cosmos that the human mind, soul, and spirit attempts to seek out. There are primordial categories that we discover again and again, whether in philosophy, religion, psychology, or even—perhaps unconsciously—in science. My relationship to these archetypal principles will always be shaped by the astrological lens through which I first encountered them on that transformative night in the temple beneath the stars. But these same archetypal principles I know have been, and will continue to be, expressed in multiplicitous and diverse form as long as there is a creative relationship between the immanent and transcendent domains.

A potent image that has come to me in many of my psychospiritual journeys is that of a prism refracting white light into an iridescent rainbow of colors. At times I have seen the white light as the undifferentiated unity of the Divine, and the spectrum of hues as the many archetypal principles, with the infinite shades of each color depicting the numberless potential manifestations of these archetypes. As for what the prism symbolizes, I've speculated that it might be the threshold of creation, Divine potential passing into ever deeper shades of immanence. At other times, I've seen the prism itself as God, with the white light as pure chaos and creativity, the rainbow spectrum again as the archetypal principles ordered out of this primordial chaos. In whatever manner this metaphoric image is specifically interpreted, what it seems to convey is a relationship between the One and the Many, depicting a divine unity of the whole sacred cosmos, and a pantheon of many principles that are emanations of that unity.

My spiritual journey was initiated on a small farm, where my embodied connection with the Earth made me question how modern humanity could ever have become so disconnected from this planet that brought us forth that we could destroy its ecosystems for our own short-term gain. From that immanent place of questioning, I was led towards a deeper understanding of historical patterns, informed by the astrological cycles of the planets. The most pivotal turn was guided by sacred medicines, leading to the encounter with the pantheon of archetypes of the Anima Mundi. The indeterminate spiritual Mystery, from my perspective, can be recognized as the Anima Mundi, the Soul of the Cosmos, refracting ever anew into the archetypal patterns that shape our very being and every perception. As I have come more and more to trust this vision of the Divine, I can hold in context our moment in the cycles of history:

although we are currently living through a period of disconnection and crisis, the sacred story continues to unfold, and where death may seem to reign, rebirth is inherently imminent—a rebirth taking place within the womb of the eternal Anima Mundi.

* * *

Questions for Discussion

1. Becca's initial transition toward embodiment came through the ecological wisdom of the Earth. In what ways are you disembodied and in need of re-embodiment? How do you understand these distinctions? What might change if farming or gardening became a fundamental part of your spiritual practice? What might the *practice* of embodiment look like for you?

2. Becca's spiritual journey deepened substantially when she began to truly pay attention to her father's work. Consider the role that your parents or wider family has played in your spiritual path. Has it been positive or negative? What familial wisdom might you be overlooking?

3. Becca's path involved not only looking down in connection to the Earth, but also looking up in connection to the astrological bodies. To what extent is this kind of *cosmic connection* also a part of your spiritual journey? What astrological wisdom might lie in wait of your discovery? Have you ever considered the heavenly bodies as a source of spiritual wisdom?

4. Becca distinguished between "participatory" and "perennialist" orientations toward spirituality and religion. Discuss the differences between these orientations. What is unique and/or significant about participatory spirituality in contrast to perennialist? Which resonates with you the most?

5. Bacca came to understand the divine mystery as the *Anima Mundi*, the soul of the cosmos. What kind of model of God does

this language suggest? If God is the soul of the cosmos, can the cosmos also be understood as God's body? Why is it important to also think of God as embodied in this way?

Sages to Explore

- Rudolf Steiner
- Richard Tarnas
- Stanislav Grof
- Arne Trettevik
- Jorge Ferrer
- Carl Jung

12: *Dissolving into the Divine*

Christopher M. Bache

Though I was a professor of religious studies for over thirty years, my understanding of God is primarily rooted not in my academic studies but in my psychedelic practice. Between 1979 and 1999, when I was thirty to fifty years old, I did seventy-three carefully planned high dose LSD sessions following a protocol developed by Stanislav Grof.[1] Isolated from the outside world, protected by a sitter, wearing eyeshades and listening to carefully selected music, I systematically shattered the boundaries of my mind, dissolving step by step into a vast ocean of consciousness. For legal reasons, I had to keep my psychedelic practice largely hidden from my colleagues at the university, but after digesting and reflecting on these experiences for twenty years, I published the story of this journey in my book, *LSD and the Mind of the Universe*.[2]

There was nothing in my background that hinted my life would take this unusual turn. Quite the opposite, in fact. I grew up in the Deep South (Vicksburg, Mississippi) in a middle class Roman Catholic family that was religiously observant but open-minded. From as early as I can

---

[1] Stanislav Grof, *LSD Psychotherapy* (Pomona, CA: Hunter House, 1980).
[2] Christopher M. Bache, *LSD and the Mind of the Universe* (Rochester, VT: Inner Traditions, 2019). After three medium dose sessions, I worked consistently at 500-600 mcg. This is a very aggressive regimen and one that I don't recommend, for reasons given in the book.

remember, I wanted to be a priest. This draw to the spiritual life did not come from my parents. It felt innate, like something I was simply born with. I entered the seminary in high school, but after four years decided that I was not cut out for celibacy and left. The pull to spiritual matters continued.

I went to the University of Notre Dame where I was fortunate enough to get into a program that let me pick my courses from across the undergraduate and graduate curriculum. I studied widely but eventually majored in theology with a focus on New Testament studies, learning Greek and Hebrew in the process. I read Carl Jung and Mahatma Gandhi, who deepened my commitment to taking responsibility for my personal shadow and work for social justice. Against the backdrop of Vietnam, I became a conscientious objector. At graduation I was given my department's award for excellence, but by then I was no longer a Catholic.

As I continued my studies at Cambridge University, my passion became the search for the historical Jesus, the scholarly movement to recover the core of Jesus' teaching from beneath the many layers that have accumulated around it in scripture. I learned the arts of form criticism, textual criticism, and redaction criticism, peeling away history in search of its deeper truths. Ironically, the historical Jesus became my way out of Christianity, for in him I found a depth of spiritual realization that was larger than Christianity.

When I came to Brown University, I shifted to studying the broad contours of western religious thought, following Christian and Jewish theology through the great minds of the Middle Ages into the fateful encounter with the Age of Enlightenment. I absorbed the philosophical and psychological revolutions of the modern mind, fell in deeper love with science, and watched it demolish theology with the sheer grandeur of the universe it was revealing. Eventually I fashioned myself into a philosopher of religion in the analytic tradition. My dissertation on the problem of religious language concluded that using language derived from our finite existence to describe an infinite God was fatally flawed. Like shining flashlights at the stars, our words may launch well but they fizzle out semantically before they reach their mark. Accordingly, I emerged from seven years of graduate school a deeply convinced agnostic with strong atheistic leanings. This is the mind I brought to my psychedelic studies—well trained in the history of religious thought, skilled in analytic discourse, and swept clean by the modern era.

I had no experience with psychedelics when I began teaching at Youngstown State University in Ohio in 1978. With my dissertation completed, I was searching for where to take my research when I found Stanislav Grof's *Realms of the Human Unconscious*,[3] and my life pivoted. In one reading Grof convinced me that LSD could be safely used in therapeutic settings not only to heal the wounds of the personal psyche but also to explore the deepest recesses of consciousness. I immediately saw the importance of Stan's work to philosophy. LSD was a doorway to a deeper engagement with the universe.

All my life I have had a passionate desire to understand how our universe works. Why are our lives the way they are? Why is there so much suffering in life? Is there a larger intelligence operating in the universe, and if so, toward what end? What is the purpose and project of existence? Despite the legal prohibitions imposed by the Controlled Substances Act in 1970, I could not turn down the opportunity to explore these questions using this new tool, and so the journey that would define the rest of my life began.

When I began my psychedelic work in 1979, it quickly dissolved my agnosticism, but it also reinforced my rejection of theism. The universe I was entering was clearly not the blind mechanical universe endorsed by mainstream science but a living universe saturated with consciousness. At the same time, this universe was so vast, so complex and intelligent that it demolished the traditional concepts of God held by the world's religions. What did these culturally embedded, historically tainted deities have to do with the infinity I was dissolving into? Very little, I decided.

In the years that followed, I expanded my understanding of Asian

---

[3] Stanislav Grof, *Realms of the Human Unconscious* (New York: Dutton, 1976).

spirituality by teaching survey courses in eastern religions and more specialized courses in Buddhism. I taught comparative mysticism to absorb the teachings of the contemplative masters from different cultural lineages. I read widely in transpersonal psychology and tried to stay current in developments in post-quantum thought. And I digested all these flows of information through the lens of my deepening psychedelic experience.

Today, my God is the Cosmos. I see all reality, both physical and spiritual reality, as the manifestation of a single intelligence whose nature is beyond our capacity to fully fathom but not beyond our capacity to experience to some degree. My metaphysical convictions fall within the boundaries of *monism* (all existence is a unitary whole), *panpsychism* (the entire physical universe is conscious), and *panentheism* (the physical universe is part of a larger divine reality). And yet these concepts don't go nearly far enough to describe the sacred reality I was entering in my sessions.

The metaphysical conclusions that flow from psychedelic experience are important, but these can be reached by any number of intellectual routes today. In our era of post-quantum theory, the innate wholeness and self-awareness of our universe is being recognized by a growing number of scientifically informed thinkers, such as Ervin Laszlo.[4] What is distinctive about psychedelics is the *experiential initiation* they give us into this universe. In deep psychedelic work one learns by *becoming*. In order to know the universe at these levels, we must temporarily become a citizen of these levels. We must become the levels themselves, and this requires more than intellectual rigor. The systematic experiential initiation into the mind of the universe signals the emergence of a new philosophical method in the West and the emergence of a new discipline—*psychedelic philosophy*.[5]

---

[4] Ervin Laszlo, *The Interconnected Universe* (River Edge, NJ: World Scientific, 1995); *Science and the Akashic Field* (Rochester, VT: Inner Traditions, 2004); *The Self-Actualizing Cosmos* (Rochester, VT: Inner Traditions, 2014); *The Intelligence of the Cosmos* (Rochester, VT: Inner Traditions, 2017).

[5] See Christopher M. Bache, *Dark Night, Early Dawn* (Albany: SUNY, 2000), ch.1. This method has ancient roots that have been well documented by scholars, from the Eleusinian mystery rites of Greece to the peyote ceremonies of Native Americans. See Paul

In my psychedelic sessions I was dissolved into a cosmic intelligence that took me in, embraced me, crushed me, and destroyed me again and again. It healed me, loved me, and eventually drew me into the Diamond Light of its innermost being. It restored my memory of what I am and what creation is. In its arms I wept and sang, died and woke anew, relived my past and pre-lived humanity's future. This intelligence instructed me ever so patiently, bringing me back month after month until it was sure I had absorbed everything it wanted me to know about a particular topic, then it moved me on. Over and over, I was stunned and humbled by the creativity and subtlety of our encounters.

As the years passed, I found myself entering a spiraling love affair with this intelligence, a Being so vast I could only describe it using the vocabulary of the Divine even while the sessions themselves were repeatedly demonstrating how limited and childlike our historical conceptions of the Divine have been. I hesitate to even call it a "Being" at all. As I have experienced it, it is the fabric of existence itself. I think of it as the generative intelligence of our universe, the Mind of the Cosmos—both transcendent source and manifest body of existence, beyond all categories of He or She, yet infinitely more than any It.

On a side note, I think sometimes we are terribly naïve in our desire to become "one with God." Are we truly prepared for the enormity of this encounter or the demands of being absorbed into dimensions of this magnitude? Science tells us that the physical universe is 93 billion light-years across, each light-year measuring a million, million miles. Our minds stagger to grasp this reality, but how much more challenging it is to grasp the Mind of this universe. And yet this ever-present Source of all that exists is what we enter when we surrender the narrow boundaries of our physical lives in deep psychedelic states.

Devereau, *The Long Trip* (New York: Penguin/Arkana, 1997); Stanislav Grof, *The Way of the Psychonaut, Vols. 1 & 2* (Santa Cruz, CA: MAPS, 2019); Ralph Metzner, *Sacred Vine of Spirits: Ayahuasca* (Rochester, VT: Park Street Press, 1997); Harold J. Ellens (ed.) *Seeking the Sacred with Psychoactive Substances. Vols. 1 & 2* (Santa Barbara, CA: Praeger, 2014); Robert Forte, *Entheogens and the Future of Religion* (San Francisco: Council on Spiritual Practices, 1997); and Huston Smith, *Cleansing the Doors of Perception* (New York: Jeremy Tarcher/Putnam, 2000).

Most contemporary philosophers, of course, hold that while human beings are conscious, the universe itself is not conscious. Galaxies are not conscious; their billions of stars are not conscious, nor are the planets that circle them. Psychedelic experience shatters this pretense and gives us firsthand experience of the fact that all matter is conscious at its core, as panpsychism asserts. Consciousness is a primary quality of existence, not a secondary quality that pops up at some point in evolution. When we follow awareness beyond the membrane of our individual minds, we enter an ocean of awareness that eventually reveals itself to encompass all of existence and to have always done so.

If we enter this ocean too quickly, we will be shattered by the enormity of the encounter. We will lose our bearings in ecstatic overload and won't be able to bring back much except speechless wonder. But if we enter these waters carefully and systematically, if we submit to the larger consciousness that receives and guides us, we will be taken in gradually, purified at deeper and deeper levels, prepared by stages for the initiations that follow, and strengthened to withstand the sheer power of the communion with infinite knowledge, infinite being, and infinite bliss (*Saccidānanda*).

I recognize the hubris and seeming arrogance of these assertions, and I apologize for taking such liberties. There is space here only for conclusions without providing supporting documentation. If I were describing only one psychedelic experience, as Aldous Huxley does in his beautiful book, *The Doors of Perception*, I might proceed differently. Then I might unpack more slowly the intimations of divinity that emerge in psychedelic states. But to describe how seventy sessions shaped my understanding of the Divine, I must take large steps.

How does a finite being who lives inside a few cubic feet of biomass survive the encounter with infinite space? How does a temporal being who lives and breathes linear time survive the transtemporal vistas of Deep Time or the timelessness of the Primal Void? They don't. To enter here, that small being must die, at least temporarily. Everything we have known ourselves to be simply perishes. Everything we have learned, loved, and hoped for is ground to dust in order to open us to life's deeper truths. The "death of self" described in our spiritual traditions is followed by other deaths, deaths that are harder to describe because they take place at levels further removed from physical existence.

After the death of my spacetime identity, there were deaths that took place at the level of the collective unconscious where what was being transcended was not my *personal* identity but my identity as a human being *per se*. In this transition the entire history of human thought with all its concepts, theories, and gods simply fell away, and nature stood naked before me once again. I entered a spacious clarity that exists beyond the field of the species-mind.[6] It was like floating in high orbit above the earth, far above the clamor and patterns of human existence. Then, after undergoing another intense death, I was taken into archetypal reality, where for a year and a half I received instruction on how reality functions at this implicate level of reality. Then another round of death and rebirth carried me into a series of ecstatic experiences of Oneness that lasted a year. This was followed by more deaths that took me rhythmically into the Diamond Luminosity for the final five years of my journey.[7]

I list these transitions only to frame how difficult it is for me to speak of the Divine given the length of my journey and its many ports of call. Which aspect of it should I focus on? Which stage of the deepening communion should I address? Should I unpack the early sessions with their dramatic storylines and dynamic interactions, or should I jump straight to the Diamond Luminosity sessions that were devoid of content save the life-changing CLARITY that Buddhism calls the "Clear Light of Absolute Reality"?

---

[6] The "species-mind" is the living consciousness of our entire species functioning as a single, integrated whole. It includes the personal psyche (both conscious and unconscious) of every human being plus Jung's collective unconscious.

[7] The "Diamond Luminosity" or "Diamond Light" is a brilliantly clear, supremely luminous radiance that exists beyond the *bardo*, beyond cyclic existence altogether. It is the crystalline body of God's innermost being. Buddhism calls it *Dharmakaya*.

The Creative Intelligence of the Universe

In all my sessions, I never encountered a personal God. Instead, my experiential horizons kept expanding as I found myself dissolving by stages into a boundless ocean of Infinite Awareness that absorbed, transmuted, and redefined all categories of divinity. All separation was extinguished in Its sacred embrace. This repeated progression into ever-deepening dimensions of existence was demonstrated in a compressed fashion in a session that took place about five years into my journey. In it I had reached a state of consciousness far beyond physical reality and was in dialogue with a vast intelligence that radically transcended my miniscule awareness. After several illuminating exchanges, I suddenly asked it, "Who am I talking to?" My session notes describe what happened next.

> With that question, my experiential field began to change, and I dropped into a new level of reality. It was as though I fell into a deeper operational level where I discovered that I was, in fact, with MYSELF. The creative impulse that had been "other" to me at the previous level was at this level Myself.
>
> This mysterious progression repeated itself many times and in many variations. It continued for hours. I would be at one level of reality far beyond physical diversity, and as I sought to know this reality more deeply, I would experience a kind of dying, a falling away, and would slip into a new level where I would discover that this duality too was but another facet of Myself. Over and over again, in detailed progressions, I was led to the same fundamental encounter.
>
> No matter how many times I died or how many different forms I was when I died, I kept being caught by this massive SOMETHING, this IT. I could not leave IT, could not escape IT, could not not be IT. No matter how many adventures I had been on, I had never stepped outside IT, never

stopped being IT. There simply was no outside to My Being. There was no other in existence.

As I moved into these levels of increasing ontological simplicity, I entered a profound stillness that reawakened a distant, vague memory. "Where have I known this before?" By following this stillness, I was guided back to what seemed like a time before creation, back to the ontological fount of creation. In this stillness, I was "with Myself" in ways that I had been long ago, but not for billions of years. It was a time of reunion, a time of being whole after a terribly long separation.[8]

This primordial Oneness has been called many things through history—the Eternal Tao, Nirguna Brahman, the Ein Sof, the Godhead, the Absolute. In *LSD and the Mind of the Universe*, I call it the Creative Intelligence of the universe. I call it my Beloved.

Over the years, this intelligence taught me many things about our universe and our life in it. It taught me that reincarnation is the higher octave of evolution, the driver of humanity's perpetual growth as we pulse back and forth across the membrane of spacetime. It taught me the *collective* dynamics of reincarnation, taking me inside the stunning beauty of humanity incarnating as a single organism. It taught me that all the experience and knowledge each of us has been gathering through our many incarnations will in time fuse into one, catapulting us permanently into a higher order of being that I call the Diamond Soul. It showed me that after countless centuries of gestation, humanity is now entering the time of its great labor. We are entering a global systems crisis that will shatter life as we have known it and drive us to our collective knees. But through this collective dark night, we are giving birth to something extraordinary. Not simply a new culture but a new order of human being, a Divine

---

[8] Session 21 in Bache, *LSD and the Mind of the Universe*, 123-24.

Child, the Future Human. History is giving birth to the Diamond Soul, and this transition will change life on our planet forever.[9]

The Final Vision

I want to end this essay by sharing the last major visionary experience I received on my journey. Coming at the end of many years of initiations, it will lack context here, but I hope it will speak to you. It is not a session of ecstatic absorption into the Divine, which would have been one way to end this chapter. Instead, it is a teaching about the nature and purpose of physical existence itself, about how life grows here, and where evolution is taking us. It does not mention God, and yet it is saturated with Divine intent. It illustrates both the price one pays for these initiations and the extraordinary adventures in consciousness that follow if one pays this price, in this case an adventure into the universe experienced within a radically expanded temporal horizon.

Session 70

For a long time after the opening preliminaries, my existence was being challenged and I was being psychologically dismembered. Familiar with this drill by now, I opened and did not resist what was happening.

My existence was being peeled away layer by layer. I kept surrendering to the process, but it never stopped. It passed levels I had known before but pressed on. I kept surrendering, but here and there I began to feel afraid. It was not that there was an "I," Chris Bache, who was afraid, for Chris Bache was already in pieces by now, but something underneath my usual identity was beginning to protest.

The process was cutting too deep.

---

[9] The visions of the birth of the Future Human began in 1991, long before global climate destabilization was on my radar.

What was happening?

I didn't understand what was happening or why.

A deeper existential fear rose.

Where was I?

Where was this going?

My sanity was at risk.

I kept waiting for the relief that comes after a major breakthrough, but today the breakthroughs were not followed by release, only more stripping away.

It was relentless.

The fear rose but did not overwhelm me. Part of me saw it and understood just enough to know that I could still choose how to meet what was happening. At a critical juncture, I made a conscious choice to surrender even more completely to this process, to let it take me deeper into this new territory than I had ever been taken before.

When I surrendered, the falling apart did not release me, as I had hoped, but instead escalated beyond measure. It reached levels of intensity beyond any understanding I can bring to it. Forces were activated that were completely new to me, even after sixty-nine sessions. Once I surrendered to the fear, it faded and was not a significant factor from that point on. The fear had simply been a boundary membrane.

In the chaos of sound, in the driving cadence of disciplined confusion, I was falling apart.

Whole parts not only of my personal being but of reality as I had known it were falling away suddenly and dramatically, as when large pieces of a glacier suddenly break off and fall into the sea. Over and over again, parts of my life fell away, then parts of life itself fell away. I was repeatedly losing all frames of reference and had just enough coherence left to recognize this fact and surrender to it again and again, plunging ever further into unknown territory. I don't know how to describe this territory beyond repeating the phrase "falling away." Being dismembered not of limb but of reality, every part of my world being ripped asunder, tossed aside. Plunging deeper and deeper into chaos.

Eventually, after a very long time, I began to realize that the process had completed itself. Completely without any reference point, I turned to explore where I was.

As in other recent sessions, I felt myself to be in my familiar world. I did not feel removed from the physical world but very much part of it. I was aware of my surroundings in the room and of my existence in these surroundings. At the same time, in my inner vision I was also seeing a lush, verdant forest with clouds moving overhead, sun streaking through and lighting up the leaves dancing in the wind. These two realities occupied the same space without complication despite their different orders of scale.

Everything was looking quite ordinary when suddenly, without the slightest effort or movement on my part, I experienced both this forest and my immediate surroundings completely differently. The forms of the forest became fluid, and everything began to shimmer and move. Time opened, and I began to experience the physical world as the rising and falling of life-forms. Another way of saying this is that time began to accelerate. First months, then years passed in seconds. This was not a hallucination but a deep excursion into how time is known in a deeper part of the universe.

I experienced the entire world as a throbbing, dynamic, living whole that was throwing up generation after generation of living beings and then reabsorbing them into itself, like waves washing up on a beach. The time expansion was enormous. In the few seconds that it takes a wave to crest and fall upon a shore, I witnessed an entire generation of human beings be born, live their entire lives, and pass away, their lives reabsorbed into the Totality, their energy forms re-assimilated and folded into the next wave as it crashed onto the shore. Generation after generation of reincarnating beings.

This was a devastating and transcendent experience simultaneously. There was no questioning or doubting what was happening. This was not a symbolic or imaginary representation of life but the real thing—life experienced from a different temporal and spatial vantage point. Reality opened, and the world of individual reference points dissolved into the larger rhythms of the Life-That-Lives-Through-Us.

If I had not been prepared for this experience by many previous encounters, it would have absolutely destroyed me. To experience from the inside the LARGER LIFE composed of all our individual lives but so far beyond them as to dwarf them in every imaginable way, to witness ten generations of human beings pass in but a minute on a Sunday afternoon, this would have shattered me had there been anything left of "me" to shatter, but after all these years there was nothing left, and so I saw life as it is.

What I was seeing and experiencing was "Samsara in the Raw"—the entire physical universe as a restless surging field of short-lived life-forms. Like the forest that lives through the constant turnover of trees rising and falling, everything in our universe is constantly turning over. Everything is temporary. Everything rises and falls over and over again. An endless succession of "births" followed by "deaths," endings blending into beginnings, nothing wasted, everything conserved. Roots completely entangled. No private lives, no private intentionality. Everything linked in time and space. A single living flow that exists at a deeper order of reality than our individual lives.

The Ocean of Existence that the temporary forms of life were rising out of and falling back into was an Ocean of Light. This Light did not overwhelm and blot out the physical universe as it had in some previous sessions. Rather, today I was watching Light manifest as physical existence. The physical world was arising from Light and returning to Light in a constant motion within multiple time frames simultaneously, some lasting seconds, some lasting centuries. From within every frame of reference possible, I saw the world as it is:

Light manifesting as Matter.
Dharmakaya manifesting as Nirmanakaya.
Heaven giving birth to Earth continuously.

It was exquisitely beautiful to witness.

Against this vast background, the following three experiences emerged:

Built for Speed

First, there was the final installment of the master story of humanity, a coda to everything that had been given before.

Underneath the rising and falling of the short-lived life-forms of physical existence were deeper FORMS that caught and structured the entire process. I experienced these FORMS to be like a riverbed through which the river of life flows in its short and turbulent cycles. This was the dominant metaphor for the process. A riverbed holds and channels the water that flows through it. In a similar manner, these FORMS channeled the life energy that flowed through them. Short-lived mini-forms (human lives) received their structure and direction from these larger FORMS. The theme of this entire sequence was: "The constantly changing manifestations of life arise on top of FORMS that change more slowly." My focus was on the FORM that was the channel for the human race, the FORM of Homo sapiens.[10]

My earlier visions of humanity's future and the Great Awakening were affirmed and commented on in a matter-of-fact way. Everything seen in previous sessions was corroborated, and now one final piece was being added. This piece moved me deeply. It felt extremely important, as though it were a vital missing piece from what I had seen before.

The missing piece was appreciating how dynamic a species we are in the larger arc of time. The constant turnover of reincarnating generations carried great significance. From my expanded time horizon, I saw that historians and theologians have taught us to think far too statically about "human nature." The constant turnover of reincarnating generations combined with the continuous accumulation of experience at this deeper centralized level means that we are carrying our collective past within us in a state of dynamic flux. Our entire history is alive within our living FORM and subject to rapid change under the right conditions.

We are an especially dynamic species precisely because each generation is so relatively short-lived while our learning as a species accumulates continuously at deeper levels, resulting in periodic shifts in our underlying FORM. In this two-level dynamic process, our species seemed to be designed for rapid transformation.

The Great Awakening that is coming is a shift in the FORM of our species, in our underlying architecture. It is

---

[10] These FORMS seemed to function something like Rupert Sheldrake's morphic fields. They gathered the learning of generations into a living blueprint of the species, a blueprint that changes and grows as the species learns. See Rupert Sheldrake, *Morphic Resonance: The Nature of Formative Causation* (Rochester, VT: Park Street Press, 2009).

the fact that we carry our psychological past in our present FORM that will allow us to transcend this past quickly IF our attention is deeply aroused. The burden of history felt comparatively light to such a being.

The net result is that human beings are built for speed. We are traveling through history with much lighter packs on our backs than traditionally thought. The failure to see this comes from the habit of thinking within too small a time frame. When we expand our time horizon even slightly to one hundred thousand years, humanity seems built for accelerated change.

What was playing itself out against the vision of the forest was also registering in my immediate surroundings. What I saw operating for the larger whole I also saw operating in my own life. I too was a transient form. Everyone and everything around me was a transient form. Our collective lives focused a life process that stretched seamlessly through time and space with not a single thread of separation anywhere.

The Diamond Maker

At one point, I saw all humanity constantly dissolving into what looked like a tangled swamp, representing the constant digesting and redigesting of human experience that is the topsoil of the reincarnation process. I then saw brilliant sparks of Diamond Light shooting up from the planet into deep space. I was witnessing the birth of a brilliant Individuality from this swamp. Not an egoic individuality but something larger and brighter. In the constant churning of space-time experience, life was growing an exquisite Soul-Individuality that continues beyond any frame of reference we can presently imagine, capable of integrating larger and larger fields of experience. I was witnessing the birth of Diamond Souls. The universe is a Diamond Maker!

We have tried to understand ourselves within a time frame that has been far too small. Nature's true time frame boggles the mind, exploding all our frames of reference. Life is a farmer growing sparks of Diamond Consciousness, and it makes little difference to It if it takes a million or a billion years for these sparks to emerge from the evolutionary cauldron It has created.

Out of all the body parts of our many historical lives, an Individuality is emerging that possesses sufficient strength to maintain continuity of awareness through the rollover of its physical forms in reincarnation. In the truest sense, there is no enduring individuality present until this point in the evolutionary process. Only at this point is the fragmentation created by repeatedly entering and leaving space-time reversed. Here, the mini-individualities of our small lives become integrated into a Soul-Individuality spanning vast stretches of time.

One sign of this emerging Soul-Individuality is that people begin to invest themselves in projects that cannot be fully realized in one lifetime. People become more "real" the more they invest themselves in projects that reach beyond the limits of their present life. The love that stretches beyond death, giving one's life that others may live, throwing one's entire being into an endeavor that will take generations to complete—all these were symptoms of the Diamond-Soul emerging in history.

The Future Human

The time frame within which all this was taking place was staggering. In a final and deeply moving portion of the session, I entered humanity's deep future again and spent time with the FORM of the being we are becoming—the Future Human. What a splendid creature! What grace and nobility! It was such a privilege to experience this being and so helpful as we enter the difficult years ahead. The people need a vision of what we are becoming, of the extraordinary beauty that is emerging from our tangled past.

I saw the Future Human standing up, and this seemed significant. Against a background of many seated Buddhas, this being was standing upright. The significance of the posture seemed to lie in its dynamism and its commitment to Earth. This was Enlightened-Humanity-in-Action. All of our knowledge, all our historical accomplishments were preserved and brought forward in enlightened activity. This penetrating glimpse transfixed me. Its beauty, grandeur, and simplicity pierced my heart. It poured a delicious nectar into me, and through me into humanity.[11]

* * *

Questions for Discussion

1. Chris' spiritual journey was deeply informed by his psychedelic practice. Consider the relationship between psychedelic experience and spiritual depth. How do you understand this relationship? Have you ever explored the spiritual resources of psychedelics? If not, are you open to trying? If so, what was your experience like?

2. For Chris, what is distinctive about psychedelics is their *experiential initiation* into that which cannot be reached through intellectual striving alone. Consider the relationship between

---

[11] Bache, *LSD and the Mind of the Universe*, 276-284, shortened here.

intellectual knowing and *experiential knowing* in light of your own spiritual journey. Has one been primary or secondary? What is the difference between the two?

3. In light of his experiences, Chris voiced that we are often "terribly naïve in our desire to become 'one with God.'" What do you think he means by this? What aspects, beliefs or dimensions of your spiritual journey have, in retrospect, been "terribly naïve"?

4. Chris said he "never encountered a personal God" during his psychedelic sessions. To what extent do you think it helpful or hindering to think of God in personal or impersonal categories? What do these categories mean when applied to God? Would you agree with Chris that God is "beyond all categories of He or She, yet infinitely more than any It"? In what ways has your own experience informed your answer?

5. Revisit Chris' extraordinary description of his final vision. What raises questions or stands out to you the most? What is deeply challenging for you? Is there something that is also comforting or inspiring? If so, why?

Sages to Explore

- Stanislav Grof
- Carl Jung
- Mahatma Gandhi

- Ervin Laszlo
- Aldous Huxley

13: We Are God's Stories

Raymond Moody

When I was a child, my family was not religious. My father was sarcastic about religion. Dad was a military officer and surgeon who served in the Pacific during World War II. His generation was not very talkative about their wartime experiences. Later, I surmised that what Dad experienced during the War must have soured him on religion.

Meanwhile, my maternal grandmother often poked gentle fun at her religious friends and their foibles. I think that the intolerant side of religious people made my grandmother pretty uncomfortable. When I was eight years old, we had a galvanized tub with two handles. One hot summer day, I filled the tub with water to splash and soak for a while. I wore uncle Fairley's fuzzy navel blue swimming trunks with a white strip on each side.

When I finished splashing, I left the dripping wet swimming trunks in the tub and dashed into the house a few feet away. My grandmother was genuinely irritated with me. She pointed to the people sitting on the front porch of the house next door. And she snapped, "Raymond, those people are Christians!" From her words and tone of voice, I gathered two things. First, we were not Christians. And, secondly, Christians must be pretty severe, stuffy people.

At that time astronomy was my favorite pastime. I built my telescope and loved gazing into the night sky and wondering what other planets might be like. I don't remember thinking or talking about God. I wouldn't call myself an atheist at that age because I did not have a positive opinion that there is no God. I suppose I was an agnostic, or thought that it is impossible to know that there is or is not a God. I focused on astronomy, not on God, and at age 18, I went to the university of Virginia to study the subject.

I took a course on Plato my first semester and immediately decided to major in philosophy, instead. Reading Plato's *Republic* was the first time I realized that some people take the idea of life after death seriously. Up to then, my sole exposure to the idea was in cartoons in magazines. I thought the drawings of clouds, pearly gates and angels were entirely a joke. But I saw that Plato was serious when he emphasized the importance of the question of an afterlife.

At the end of the *Republic*, Plato recounted a story of a warrior who was apparently killed in battle. However, the warrior revived spontaneously during his funeral. The warrior told the startled spectators that he had left his body and visited another realm during his presumed death. I asked my professor about the story, and he said that such experiences were well known to early Greek philosophers. The philosophers studied cases of people who reported profound visions when they almost died.

Plato was inclined to accept that the experiences were real. However, some other philosophers discounted them. For instance, Democritus thought that things in the world are made of minute, invisible bits he called atoms. Democritus explained the experiences of people who survived death in terms of residual biological activity in the body—for there is no such thing as an exact moment of death.

That was the first I ever heard of what we now know as near-death experiences. I had no idea that these experiences are also common in the modern world. However, in 1965, three years later, I met a living person who reported a near-death experience. Dr. George Ritchie was then a professor of psychiatry at the University of Virginia. The experience

George had while he was clinically dead changed his life and the lives of many other people, including mine.

In December 1943, George was a recruit in the Army at Camp Barkeley, Texas. George contracted double lobar pneumonia and was pronounced dead for nine minutes. A doctor resuscitated him by injecting adrenaline directly into his heart. George said that when his heart stopped beating, he left his body. He found himself in the presence of a being of bright light and complete, loving compassion who George identified as Christ. Christ guided George though a vivid panoramic review of everything he had ever done in his life.

Dr. Ritchie was very generous and often lectured to student groups. I went to one of his lectures, and it was a turning point in my life. Hearing George that night was the first time I ever consciously felt and experienced the spirit of the divine.

After that night I continued studying philosophy and received my PhD in the subject in 1969. I became a philosophy professor and soon I was hearing accounts of near-death experiences from students and colleagues. In 1972, I went to medical school and received my MD in 1976. Afterward, I served as a resident in psychiatry and eventually worked as a forensic psychiatrist. Throughout my career, I continued to interview people about their near-death experiences. The thousands of people I interviewed shared with me the encounters they had with God as they were out of their bodies, hovering on the edge of death.

God shines through people's stories as a powerfully loving, compassionate, insightful, humorous, utterly delightful and still deeply mysterious presence. I did not have a religious background and I have read very little of the Bible. I'm not interested in persuading anyone else of my own views and understanding of God. I offer these thoughts on God only because I know there are many people out there who are like me. They are looking for God and yet they are not interested in organized religion and they just don't relate to the Bible. I met many such individuals during the fifty years I have been lecturing on near-death experiences.

My message to them is that religious people and Bible believers don't have a monopoly on God or the Bible.

God Doesn't "Exist"

"Do you believe that God exists?" People sometimes ask me that question. And when they do, I always reply, "No, absolutely not!" Then I explain what I mean.

I, Raymond Moody, am a limited human being. I am beset by a host of weaknesses, faults, deficiencies, and failings. Any belief I could possibly form about God, the Supreme Being, would be bound to be off-base in one direction or another. My "beliefs" are irrelevant to God.

Besides, consider the question again. "Do you believe that God exists?" The emphasis of that sentence falls on the word "exists" rather than on God. We think that by drawing a mental boundary line around God, we can contain and confine God within our human conceptual system. And one of the most common ways of attempting this is saying that "God exists." However, the trouble is that God is too great to be captured or enclosed within a concept such as "existence."

Some people get into endless debates with others as to whether or not God "exists." I have known people whose main activity in relationship to God is thinking, talking, and arguing about whether or not God exists. Sometimes, I suspect that this activity is actually their way of keeping distance from God or trying to keep God from getting too close. Better to ruminate on abstractions like "existence" and "belief," they may feel, than risk getting up close and personal with the Supreme Being.

As a university professor of philosophy, I loved teaching logic and critical thinking. "Existence" is a central concept in logic and it would take me about an hour to explain the logical concept of existence and show how to sympathize with that concept. But that would not help you or me or anyone else in their personal search for God.

Philosophers have said some interesting and enlightening things about existence. For instance, the great Immanuel Kant said that existence is not a predicate. That is, saying a thing exists is not like attributing a particular property to it. J.L. Austin, my favorite twentieth century philosopher, also made an enlightening remark about existence. Austin said, "Existing is not something things do, like breathing, only quieter."

Neither the concept of "existence," nor its contrasting polar opposite concept of "non-existence," are serviceable for thinking about the Supreme Being. Of course, this sounds abstruse, and that is my point. I don't approach thinking about God by invoking abstract concepts like existence, non-existence or belief. Instead, I approach thinking about God in terms of my interpersonal relationships. I don't say, "I believe God exists." Rather, I say, "I have a personal relationship with God." I think God participates in our interpersonal relationships.

Love and the Purpose of God

Life After Life is the book I wrote in 1974 to describe my research into people's near death experiences. I telephoned Dr. Ritchie in September of that year to ask for permission to dedicate my book to him. He replied, "Well, that's very nice. But I would prefer you dedicate the book to the Christ who gave me this experience."

This is why the dedication to *Life After Life* reads, "To George Ritchie, M.D., and through him, to the One whom he suggested." That brief phone call was the only contact I had with George since 1965, when I first heard of his experience. *Life After Life* was published in the November of 1975 and I graduated from medical school shortly thereafter, in January of 1976.

Early in my psychiatry residency, I figured out that most people chase something. I saw that some of my patients were chasing power. However, it seemed that it didn't satisfy them once they got it. Others were chasing sex in an endless runaround. Yet others were chasing fame and it seemed that what they were really looking for was self-esteem—feeling better about themselves. They seemed to imagine that if a lot of other people liked and admired them, they might like themselves, too. Some of my patients were chasing money. Some got it and other didn't. And at age seventy-six with two kids, I wish I had chased money too at some point in my earlier life. But I was preoccupied with teaching philosophy and learning about medicine psychiatry.

One day I reported my observation to my very wise supervisor. "John, I notice that everybody seems to be chasing something. I'm feeling a little uneasy about myself because I'm not chasing anything. I enjoy what I'm doing now."

John smiled his comforting, understanding smile. "Raymond," he asked, "How old were you when you finished your doctoral degree in philosophy?"

"I was twenty-four," I replied.

He went on, "Then, as I remember, you taught philosophy for three years. After that you went to medical school. So how old were you when you finished your second doctoral degree?"

"I was thirty-one," I said, and somewhere in mid-sentence I realized that I was chasing knowledge. Yes, I have spent my life chasing knowledge and it has been a satisfying and fulfilling quest for me. For when I was about eight years old, I realized that as much as I loved knowledge, I would never have much of it compared to the cosmic scale. Still, the relative paucity of human knowledge somehow enhances the joy that comes from the little of it we can get in this life.

The legions of people I interviewed about their near-death experiences had been chasing all those things too, before their personal encounters with God. Afterward, however, whatever they were chasing before, they came to a common understanding. They agreed that what this life seems to be about, in large part, is learning to love.

This understanding is thrust upon them through holographic, panoramic reviews which simultaneously focus on every detail of their earthly lives. In panoramic life reviews, people view the details of their lives through the lens of love—God's love. Many revisit their lives in the presence of a bright light—a personal being composed of light—or love. In that transcendent state, they say the light is identical with sheer, indescribable love and compassion. They identify the personal being of light as God, or Christ, or an angel. The identifying word varies from individual to individual depending partly, it seems, on their religious, spiritual, or cultural traditions. Even so, whatever identifying term they use, their descriptions converge. They encounter a divine being of light of complete compassion who knows everything about them and loves them totally and completely. Everyone says that the love they felt from the light of God surpassed anything that we experience as love in this life. And the contrast between God's love and love experienced in this world is too great to be described, or put into words.

When I lecture on near-death experiences, people often ask me, "What kind of love are we supposed to be learning to give while we are living in this world?"

That is a good question. "Love" is not just a descriptive term, it is also a normative, prescriptive, or evaluative term. When we say we "love" someone or something we are thereby placing a positive value on that person, place, or thing. People use the same word "love" when they say "I love Jane," "I love New York," or "I love pie and ice cream." Because we associate a positive value with "love," it feels good and inspiring when we hear that people who report near-death experiences tell us that the purpose of life is to learn to love. That certainly gives us something to aspire to in this life. Nevertheless, the word has a wild, wide array of different meanings and uses. So it is with near-death experiences: what people tell us can be confusing, too. What they say is inspiring, but for it to be a practical guide for life, we need more detail. What kind of love exactly are they talking about?

Romantic love comes naturally to many people's mind when they hear the word. That is the kind of love that we most often see played out on the screen when we go to the movies. Romantic love has been characterized as a religion consisting of two people. "Roman" is a French word for "novel." That contains a clue to what romantic love is. Romantic love has a story attached to it. People who experience romantic love love to tell the story of how they met and got to know each other.

Companionate love is the love that grows between two people through the companionship they share over stretches of time. Passionate love involves and emphasizes the dimension of motivation, or intense motivation. Commitment is another dimension of love—two people mutually committing themselves to stay together and help each other through thick and thin, through and good times and the bad times.

"Storage" (a Greek term) is a wonderous form of love that used to be common in America but is vanishing from today's society. When we were largely an agricultural and rural nation, practically everybody knew what "storage" was. I learned the term when I was an undergraduate philosophy student studying ancient Greek. And I immediately understood it because of instances of it in my own family.

In an earlier, rural America, kids from adjacent farms would often grow up together as playmates, friends, and companions. Their parents owned farms that were next to each other, so geographical destiny put a boy and a girl together. With nobody else around for miles and miles, they knew each other from birth and go to know each other well. Playmates became lifelong friends before there was any thought of sex. They formed an unbreakable bond before they were even aware of sex. Relationships like that just naturally evolved into committed, companionate marriages.

My Aunt Dwight and Uncle Clifford had exactly that type of marriage. I visited them frequently on their farm when I was a kid and they taught me many valuable life lessons. But when Uncle Clifford died, that too was pretty much the end for Aunt Dwight too. She was never the same again.

I have been guiding people through grief in my practice for decades. I have come to see that the experience of grief depends partly on what type of love existed between two people. I think grief is particularly difficult in cases of storage love. Often, when one of two people dies, the other follows soon thereafter.

So love is a wonderful, multifaceted, complex thing. I have been going on and on about love because of what people with near-death experiences tell us. They said that during their life reviews they discovered that the purpose of this life is to learn to love. But what kind of love do they mean?

To me, life reviews are perhaps the most interesting elements of people's near-death experiences. After they left their bodies, time came to a standstill and a panorama appeared around them of everything they had done in their life. They experienced every action in review but not just from the perspective they had at the time the action took place. Instead, they also revisited the action from the perspectives of the people with whom they had interacted. Hence, when they reviewed scenes in which they had treated someone else harshly, they directly felt the pain their action had caused. Or in scenes in which they had treated others with loving kindness, they directly and emphatically experienced the good feelings their actions had created.

In these reviews, God was aware of every action and prompted the person with a question, though the question was not in words. Rather, God directed a thought to the person. People invariably put the question into words as something like, "How have you learned to love?"

Whatever appeared in the panoramic review, people felt that God loved them for themselves, completely and totally. The situation itself naturally made people want to be that same way. People generally told me that God did not judge them during their experience of the review. God's purpose seemed to be education, not judgment.

Life reviews during near-death experiences are suffused with God's light and love. People with transcendent near-death experiences return with a conviction that learning to love is the essential meaning and purpose of life. Yet they often find it difficult to adhere to that standard while living in this world. Even my friend George Ritchie, the finest person I ever knew, complained of his problem, "Raymond, this experience makes your humanity even more of a burden, in a way." What George meant was that even after seeing the vital importance of love, we are still human beings and often lack love. And that does not change just because of a life review during a near-death experience.

What does change, however, is someone's underlying motivation.

After life reviews during their near-death experiences, people are more strongly motivated to change. They generally become more loving in their daily lives. During my career, I got to know thousands of people with stories of their near-death experiences. I think that they do very well in their quests. Many of them recounted to me that after their experiences they occasionally felt a longing or intense nostalgia or homesickness for the love of God.

I suspect that God's love for us is multidimensional in ways we are incapable of comprehending or even imagining while living this life. God's love has all sorts of manifestations and powers that are beyond the reach of the mind. However, one thing does seem clear and demonstrable. Specifically, God's love for us is somehow tied to our capacities to create, tell, and appreciate stories, or narratives.

God's Stories

God made people, Elie Wiesel said, because God loves stories. Wiesel, a deep and soulful man, survived Auschwitz to win the Nobel Prize for literature after the war. I am awed by his humanity and presence of mind amidst the horrible ordeals he suffered. His life path led him to realize that God loves to participate in our life stories. By contrast, I have led a pampered life. Hence, it is with real humility that I concur with his thought. For I came to that same conclusion by a different path.

God loves tuning into our life stories. From what people say about their life reviews, I gather that God follows every individual's life story as it unfolds. Furthermore, not only does God follow the nuances of every person's story, God follows those stories as they weave together through their interconnection. God sees an immense interweaving of life stories that is invisible to any single person. God views the whole in a single sweep. And every person's life is connected through God to every other person's life.

Life reviews pertain to an ancient philosophical puzzle known as the problem of personal identity. Around 600 BCE, in Greece, a man named

Hermotimus gained fame for his ability to get out of his body at will. Hermotimus would leave his body and travel to distant locations to see what was happening there. Hence, early Greek philosophers grasped that we consist of minds (or souls) and bodies. So they wanted to figure out which one determines our personal identity. Are we essentially souls or bodies?

Plato eventually propounded the theory that personal identity resided in our immaterial, immortal souls. The physical body, Plato said, is constantly changing and has no part in stable reality. The body, Plato thought, is a vessel or vehicle of the soul which dissolves when the soul leaves it. In his sterner frame of mind, Plato claimed that the body is a jailhouse or prison of the soul. And he portrayed dying people as joyous escapees, as long as they had led a life of pursuing knowledge as wisdom. Philosophy, Plato said, is rehearsal for dying.

In the seventeenth century, Plato's theory that personal identity resided in an immaterial soul fell out of favor. Certainly, the notion of an immortal, immaterial soul feels warm and fuzzy to us. Nonetheless, philosophers like Thomas Hobbes argued that the idea of an immaterial soul is meaningless and incoherent, upon careful analysis. The idea that the immaterial soul is not an intelligible concept took hold in western thought.

Philosopher John Locke defined personal identity in terms of memory. Locke said that the essence of a person's identity consists of that person's memories. In other words, the self consists of that person's memoires. David Hume then took a more radical step. He maintained that when he looked most deeply into what he thought of as his self, he never could find any persistent, underlying entity. When he looked within, Hume said, he could find only passing impressions. This view of the self as a mental and linguistic fiction, or illusion, is practically a tenet of today's psychology and neuroscience.

I have a different take on the problem of personal Identity. I say that we are our life stories. Someone's personal identity is ultimately constituted by that individual's life story. Moreover, God is tuned in to every person's life story. And God sees all our life stories interweaving.

The nature of consciousness itself shows how essential narratives, or stories, are for individual personal identity. The moment a significant new event occurs in a person's life, the conscious mind acts to fold that event into the person's ongoing life story. Hence, personal consciousness is pointed in the direction of a continuing narrative of that person's life. That is, the conscious mind focuses on keeping a narration flowing of that person's life as it unfolds.

A large part of personal consciousness comes in story form. Much of the mind is occupied with keeping track of people's stories, or narratives. That someone's conscious mind keeps track of that individual's life story is remarkable enough, but that same person's mind keeps track of a lot of others individual life stories as well. Many of those stories are those of people the individual knows as relatives, friends, or acquaintances. Yet numerous other life stories of historical personages, public figures, or even fictional characters are also held within that same, single, individual's conscious mind.

Story consciousness makes up a large portion of ordinary consciousness. The physical world may be made of atoms, but the human world is made of stories. And God watches and keeps track of and participates in all the life stories that ever were or will be. As Elie Wiesel said, God made people because God loves stories. So I think that we are God's stories.

I think some people realize this for themselves as they grow older. I once worked for a year as a geriatric psychiatrist serving elderly patients in a university town. Some of my patients suffered from dementia due to Alzheimer's disease, Pick's disease, or other conditions. However, the majority of the patients who came to the clinic were cognitively sharp. They were generally accomplished, distinguished members of the local community. They came to see me primarily for situational stress, or sometimes because of loneliness, or to have someone to talk to.

As elderly people tend to do, my patients often looked back and reflected on the lives they led and reminisced. Repeatedly during that year, I heard the same poignant remark from distinguished elders. They commented that the older they became, the stronger an uncanny impression developed that their life had been a script, story, play, or movie. That idea may seem unusual when you first hear it, but it is actually a normal developmental phase of aging. My patients' observations in no way resembled psychotic thinking or delusions.

At first, I wondered whether what they were telling me might be a local tradition, or folklore. Perhaps it was a folk belief in that area that aging people begin to view their life in retrospect as a script. Then, years later, I heard renowned mythologist Joseph Campbell say that same thing about his experience of aging. Subsequently, I heard this comment from elderly people in various parts of the United States, Canada, and Europe. So I assume that this is a fairly common experience reflecting elderly people. I also suspect that many people reading this will be able to confirm this observation for themselves.

In the meantime, a careful logical thinker would have reason to accuse me of committing a fallacy. In fact, it would be one of the logical fallacies that Aristotle identified in his pioneering work on patterns of fallacious reasoning. Specifically, an objector might argue that I have taken on a limited aspect of culture—the theatre—and used it to characterize all human reality. That would be a fallacious use of a metaphor—a figure of expression—by treating it as a literal meaning. I would be saying (metaphorically) that life is a play while acting as though I were talking literally. I understand the objection, but I think that things happened the other way around. The idea that life is a story did not arise from metaphorically extending the idea of the theatre. Rather, I think the theatre arose from the idea that aging people develop that their lives have been scripts or stories.

In ancient Athens, a chorus performed yearly during a traditional harvest festival. The chorus sang stories of old Greek heroes. During one performance, for reasons unknown, a performer stepped forward from the chorus and spoke his own lines. When Thespis violated this entrenched tradition, it created a sensation. The crowd went wild and demanded more of this new exciting form of entertainment. Competitiveness was among the more conspicuous traits of the ancient

Greek mentality. Hence, when the new entertainment stirred in the crowd, the king degreed a contest. A race was on to see who could write the best play to perform in the newborn theatre. The big winners, over several decades, were Aeschylus, Sophocles, and Euripides. The three gained immortal fame and their plays are still performed and studied today. Theatres had once been temples of gods and goddesses, but they soon gained the status of a profession.

Why did that event take place so rapidly? What gave the theatre its instant and inherent appeal? Aeschylus, Sophocles, and Euripides—three wise men—thought about and reflected on human life. Their wisdom still shines through their plays many centuries later. They probably realized that old people look back on their lives as scripted stories. That is something that observant, reflective people realize for themselves. The Greek dramatists could have observed that as easily as we observe it today. Flattening the ground in an area created a place out in the open to act out life stories for people to see.

That is a spontaneous, smooth, natural process of development. The process is grounded in the insight that elderly people view their lives in retrospect as scripted stories. Each individual is conscious of a personal life story as it unfolds. Why do narratives occupy such a large portion of the conscious mind? Is the narrative dimension of consciousness necessary for understanding God or communicating with God? Do we need narrative consciousness to have relationships with God?

I don't think that stories and narrative consciousness are the only means of understanding God, or communicating with God or having relationships with God. Certainly, there are additional means of doing so. People also encounter God in near-death experiences or in mystical visions, for example. Even so, many religious people, perhaps the majority, depend on stories for thinking about God and relating to God. For instance, millions of worshipers base their faith primarily on the Bible, and to a significant degree, the Bible is made up of stories or narratives.

So again I say: we are God's stories. We have a narrative connection with God, along with some other kinds of connections. And when we die, we review our entire life story in the loving presence of God. In God, we see connections between our life stories and the life stories of other people we knew while we were alive.

A few years ago, I lectured on near-death experiences at a Hindu ashram. During my lecture, I discussed my ideas about personal identity, life reviews, and life as a story. After my lecture, the swami of the ashram spoke up and told me that Hindus had reached the same conclusion. Life is a drama or play and the world is a kind of theatre—or a spiritual theatre.

I can step back and view my own life as a story or play, but it is hard to maintain that perspective over a long period of time. After all, life is intrinsically immersive. I am a self-conscious subject of experience who is immersed in my own story. I can grasp that fact by mentally distancing myself and taking a narrative stance on my life. Then, I can sustain that perspective in a kind of philosophical reverie or trance-like state consciousness. Soon, though, some personal annoyance intrudes and I am immersed again in the details—sometimes the irritating details—of my story.

Life comes at us relentlessly, and often bursts in unbidden on our most insightful philosophical reflections. Nevertheless, what we glimpse briefly but repeatedly in our "Aha!" moments can eventually settle lastingly in our minds. A bi-level state of awareness is attainable in which someone can view their life as God's story while experimentally immersed in that life.

An idea can be "good to think with," as the Greek philosophers like to say. They would entertain an idea just because thinking about it might engender new and interesting insights or discoveries. The idea of a life as a story is good to think with when we investigate the question of life after death.

Reincarnation and the Problem of Evil

Philosopher David Hume said that reincarnation is the only view of the afterlife a philosophically-minded person could contemplate. Maybe

Hume thought so because he knew that narratives, or stories, are essential for understanding human nature. Reincarnation is perhaps the most story-centered conception of life after death.

Supposedly, when we finish one life story we die and go through some incomprehensible process in another dimension. We then emerge from that other dimension and begin a new life story centered in a new body and usually in a different locale. When that new story ends in death of the body, we repeat the incomprehensible process culminating in another rebirth. Authoritative sources disagree concerning how many cycles an individual must complete and why. They also disagree concerning what the individual's fate will be upon completing the final life story.

Earlier, I mentioned people who like to think and argue about whether or not God "exists." One topic they frequently argue about is what is known as the problem of evil. Presumably, God is loving, God knows everything, and God can do anything. Why then, some ask, do terrible things happen? The argument is often raised to suggest that God does not "exist." Reincarnation, together with a story perspective on life, can put a different spin on this.

Suppose you contracted an infectious illness that required you to live alone on an island for ten years. You are flown to the island in a cargo plane carrying a supply of food, water, and medicine to last a decade. Happily, there is enough cargo space for a video player and, let's say, a supply of 5,000 movies. Given that scenario, would you choose all comedies?

Almost everyone I've asked that question has answered "No!" Then I ask, "Would you also choose some tragedies?" And everyone answers, "Yes!" Then, I ask, "When you are alone on the island watching a tragedy, would you be crying?" And again, everyone answers, "Yes, I would be." After all, crying is the emotional response we expect to experience when witnessing a tragedy.

We choose to watch a tragedy understanding well that we will be upset, distressed, sad, and crying while we do so. We also understand beforehand that watching a tragedy will be a self-contained, time-limited experience. The experience will be over before too long and we will get through it alive. We might even anticipate experiencing what Aristotle called catharsis, a discharge or release of pent-up negative emotions.

Imagine yourself in another dimension, the afterlife realm, preparing for your next incarnation into this world. Imagine all sorts of life stories spread out before you and you have some degree of input into what your next life will be. And you know that whatever life story you enter will be a time-limited, temporary experience. You will live that life, die, and return to the afterlife realm. You know that most if not all life stories include some degree of strife, heartbreak, distress, sadness, tragedy, and suffering. You understand that entering a life story, you become immersed in it and forget that it is one of God's own.

That is the picture Plato and others painted of a higher dimension of life from which our consciousness emerges at birth into this world. Of course, in reality the words prompt us to try and imagine the unimaginable. That higher dimension defies the mind's inbuilt system of time-space coordinates. Nevertheless, the picture accords well with the sense reflective elders develop that life is somehow a script.

Plato said that event boundaries ordinarily keep that higher dimension separate from this life. You experience event boundaries many times. Suppose you are in your living room and you decide to fetch something from the kitchen. Then as soon as you walk through the kitchen door you forget what you went in there to do. Similarly, when we emerge into this world, we forget the prelude to our life story that occurred in another state of consciousness.

Projecting myself mentally into that prior state, I can easily imagine choosing a life story full of hardships and difficulties. That is not to say that I would delight in those hardships when living amid them. No, I would be protesting, agonizing, sobbing, wishing they would go away. That is what I signed up for to begin with, then forgot about it. In that prior state, I had an education plan or even an interesting experience in mind. People stand in line for a long time to get onto a roller coaster. Yet they know full well that when they are zooming along upside down at ninety miles an hour, they won't want to be there.

I can imagine choosing to experience many different life stories full of all sorts of miseries, perplexities, and challenges, for educational purposes. Even if that higher dimension allowed me to choose only a single life story, I can't say I would necessarily choose a comedy. I might want the most interesting or instructive life story. For I would understand in advance that the story is time-limited and will end in my returning to my place of origin.

While billions of people live in cultures that officially subscribe to the concept of reincarnation, billions of others live in cultures that subscribe to a different concept in which life is a one-shot deal. According to the latter, the afterlife is a kind of cosmic justice system of rewards and punishments in heaven and hell. I think that system is meaningless and incoherent. God sees a much bigger picture than constricted human ideas of justice and injustice and retribution and revenge. I believe God loves and educates, rather than dispenses justice.

The Logic of Nonsense

Dr. Seuss's books of nonsense for children have sold 600 million copies all around the world. Lewis Carroll's classic nineteenth century works of children's nonsense—*Alice in the Wonderland* and *Through the Looking Glass*—continue to entertain multitudes of readers worldwide. And nonsense is for adults, too.

Angelic singers Ella Fitzgerald's and Louis Armstrong's jazz songs consisted of improvised nonsense syllables. Their performances transported enthralled listeners to blissful, almost otherworldly states of consciousness. Doo-wop songs that were popular in the 1950s used nonsense as the main line or for harmony. They combined nonsense with meaningful words into a unified whole. Doo-wop songs can induce trance-like states of consciousness.

Consciousness-raising shaman songs were constructed much like doo-wop songs. Shaman songs were made up of nonsense syllables and meaningless refrains put together with elements of meaningful and intelligible language. Singing these songs transported shamans into ecstatic states of awareness that they experienced as they crossed over into the spirit world. Nonsense plainly has a transcendent dimension.

At first, the idea of using nonsense for communicating with God may seems shocking and counterintuitive. Yet upon reflection we remember that nonsense is an ancient, still thriving practice for carrying on a living relationship with God. Glossolalia, or speaking in unknown tongues, is associated with the Christian faith for the most part, but it is also practiced in other religious and spiritual traditions. Linguistically, glossolalia is the spontaneous utterance of a stream of nonsense syllables drawn from the speaker's own language. I tried glossolalia myself and was awed by the inspiriting unifying state of consciousness it created. I can easily imagine that such an uplifted state could open someone to an experiential encounter with God.

Nonsense also enters into central theological concepts of various religions. Christianity's doctrine of the Trinity is a case in point. According to the Trinity, God is one, but in three persons: the Father, Son, and Holy Ghost. Though the doctrine is vital to many believers, in reality the Trinity has no intelligible meaning. One and three are distinct numbers and to say that one is identical to three is unintelligible nonsense. The Trinity is nonsense because it breaks the rules of arithmetic and destroys the meaning of numbers. In medieval times, though, the Trinity was not so much a doctrine as a kind of logico-spiritual mental exercise. Wrestling with the perplexities of the Trinity by thinking about it logically was a way of contemplating the identity of God. The idea was to generate insights into the nature of God by thinking rigorously and logically about the paradoxes of the Trinity.

In that respect, the Trinity bears some resemblances to a Zen Buddhism's koans. Koans include some nonsensical and unintelligible questions such as, "What is the sound of one hand clapping?" A Zen master chooses an appropriate koan to assign to a student. The student tries at first to answer the illogical questions by applying logical reasoning. That won't work, though, and eventually the futile task breaks the students mind through transcendent states that lie beyond logic and reasoning.

Excessive preoccupation with logic and reason can keep us distant from God. Nonsense can break down fixation on logic and reason and move us closer to God. The mind we have does not get us far toward comprehending God. But we can empower our minds to think logically about unintelligible nonsense, and that leads us a little closer to comprehending God. Every advance in consciousness helps us to be more amendable and open to a relationship with God.

For me, learning to love in personal relationship with God is the defining purpose of life. But many other people, I know, feel a need to think as deeply as they can about God. They try logical reasoning as a path toward comprehending God. Some great thinkers who took that path arrived at a barrier of unintelligibility. They came to see that from the standpoint of literal meaning, talk about God is nonsensical. Which is fine, because I think the idea of God *is* nonsense. At first, that statement sounds like an insult. Or, the statement could be another way of saying God does not "exist." Actually, however, neither of those analyses bears scrutiny.

"The idea of God is nonsense" is a statement about the limits of the human mind. Calling the idea of God unintelligible nonsense is a reminder of what the mind cannot comprehend. God transcends all the conceptual systems that the intellect may use to make sense of reality. And isn't that exactly what reflective people have always thought about God in the first place? It is because attempts to comprehend God with reason are futile, and our intellectual mind cannot corral God within concepts and abstractions, that I believe embracing nonsense as a valid dimension of thought and communication helps ease the way to cherishing God's companionship.

Nonsense and the Reality of Life After Death

During near-death experiences, the conscious mind crosses over into a transcendent realm. People who absorb principles of the logic of non-sense can carry those principles when they cross to the next life. That empowers the mind to interact cognitively with a near-death experience in a new, more effective way. That will influence how a person puts their experience into words, upon being revived. In other words, learning the logic on nonsense will affect how someone recounts their near-death experience in the future. In effect, advance knowledge of logical principles of nonsense alleviates the problem of ineffability associated with near-death and mystical experience.

This has already happened. A renowned artist and scientist partici-pated in one of my nonsense seminars. Several years later he almost died from a severe case of influenza. During his ordeal he underwent three cardiac arrests and had profound near-death experiences. He said that when he was on the other side his mind went back to the nonsense sem-inar. From that vantage point, he realized why knowledge of principles of nonsense is necessary for comprehending how the next life is related to this life.

A rational proof of life after death will not come from a single indi-vidual working alone. Nor will a proof come from a small team of ded-icated researches. Instead, many people need to participate in a large collected research project. Together, we can step across the mental and logical frontier that separate this life from the life hereafter. I am pro-posing a collective study of near-death experiences and the afterlife in which anyone can participate. My study first prepares participants' mind to think with a new logic about life after death; then, they will be able to describe their subsequent near-death experiences utilizing the tools they have learned.

My recent book, *Making Sense of Nonsense*, brings all my research together in a single volume. It also includes the exercises that were an integral part of my course and seminars. *Making Sense of Nonsense* serves as a guidebook for readers participating in my collective study of near-death experiences and life after death.

You can join the collective study by reading the book and completing the exercises. That will reformat your mind and enable you to think logically about things that are unintelligible and nonsensical. This process has many practical benefits. Learning the logic of nonsense improves critical and analytical reasoning and inspires creative thinking. Knowing the logic of nonsense is highly useful for writers, teachers, psychologist, physicians, advertisers, and professionals in numerous other fields. The process also prepares you to be a better observer and investigator of any near-death experience you might have in the future. Together, we could enlighten humankind on the greatest, deepest mystery of life.

What is my personal stance toward the afterlife in light of my several decades of research? I think that a dying individual's personal consciousness emerges from the physical world and finds itself in a larger, more inclusive sphere of reality. In that larger sphere, personal consciousness no longer orients itself by where it is in space or time. Instead, in that other sphere, there is a different coordinate system. By that system, personal consciousness appears to orient itself by love and by information or knowledge. I can condense and summarize the above: I think there is a life after death.

I could not and would not make that statement in a void. That is, I would not make the statement unless there were publicly confirmable and understandable concepts that explain and support the statement. Specifically, the logic of nonsense forms the conceptual background of my statement. Others may agree or disagree with my judgment that there is life after death. The logic of nonsense is a common reference point by which such agreements or disagreements can be judged or mediated. And I claim that the logic of nonsense will prove superior to ordinary logic for mediating such controversies.

I am confident that collective research will yield valuable results. Eventually, this collective study of near-death experiences will lead to better rational comprehension of life after death. Yet rational comprehension of the afterlife will still leave us a long way from rational comprehension of God. God subsumes reason, but reason cannot subsume God.

God Is Bigger Still

God is a far greater and deeper mystery than life after death. And just as God is bigger than the Bible and God is bigger than existence itself, God far surpasses the life beyond death. But additional rational insight into near-death experiences and life after death might also give us more insight into God.

A wonderous, comforting picture of God emerges from people's stories of near-death experiences. They reveal God's nature as a wise, loving companion and counsellor and a compassionate educator. God is definitely someone you would want to be with forever, judging from people's stories of their near-death experiences.

God's presence and accessibility to us are steeped in paradox. God transcends this life. Yet God is also present and accessible to us in this life. God even transcends the next life. Yet studies of near-death experiences make it seem that God is somehow more immediately present and more directly accessible in the next life. Hopefully, our collective study of near-death experiences might someday make God's presence more immediate in this world.

In the meantime, seek a richer, fuller relationship with God. Don't feel that you have to be formal, solemn, stilted or ceremonial around God. Laugh and have a good time. Open up, relax, pray, surrender, and talk things over with God as though you were talking to an old friend. Go to God with your joys and with your sorrows. Try it for a while; make it a regular practice. Observe, reflect, and watch what happens. Perhaps nothing will; perhaps everything will. Either way, you will be enlightened. Learning about God is a process that goes on throughout this life and into the next.

* * *

Questions for Discussion

1. Research on near-death experience was central to Raymond's personal and professional journey. To what extent is an interest in life after death also a part of your spiritual journey? Have you ever had what you would describe as a near-death experience? If so, what was it like? Why is the question of life after death important for the spiritual journey?

2. In speaking about "life reviews" during near-death experiences, Raymond said that "God's purpose seemed to be education, not judgment." What changes when God is pictured as an educator rather than a judge? In reviewing your own life, has it been a process of education? If so, education about what?

3. For Raymond, the data of near-death experiences reveal that life is essentially a process of "learning how to love." What have you learned about love in your life? Love also comes in different forms and expressions. What *kind* of love has been most important for you?

4. For Raymond, what is the significance of reincarnation for thinking about the problem of evil? What changes spiritually when you have many lives and not just one? Have you ever considered that you may have *chosen* the narrative or story that you are living out? What do you think about this idea?

5. Raymond insisted that preoccupations with logic and reason can actually "keep us distant from God." Instead, he proposes the "logic of nonsense" as a means of approaching and understanding the data of near-death experiences and the reality of spiritual or mystical experience. In what ways has nonsense been a part of your journey? Why is the logic of nonsense important for thinking about God?

Sages to Explore

- Plato
- Democritus
- George D. Ritchie
- Immanuel Kant
- J.L. Austin
- Hermotimus
- Thomas Hobbes
- John Locke
- David Hume
- Joseph Campbell

- Aristotle
- Aeschylus
- Sophocles
- Euripides
- Dr. Seuss
- Lewis Carroll
- Ella Fitzgerald
- Louis Armstrong
- Elie Wiesel

Contributor Bios

Andrew M. Davis is a process philosopher, theologian, and scholar of cosmological wonder. He is program director for the Center for Process Studies where he researches, writes, and organizes conferences on various aspects of process-relational thought. An advocate of metaphysics and meaning, he approaches philosophy as the endeavor to systematically think through what reality must be like because we are a part of it. He is author, editor, and co-editor of several books including *Mind, Value, and Cosmos: On the Relational Nature of Ultimacy* which was nominated for the 2022 Book Prize of the International Society of Science and Religion. Follow Andrew's work at https://www.andrewmdavis.info/.

Beverly Lanzetta is an independent contemplative scholar, spiritual teacher, and author of books on global spirituality, the mystical path of the feminine, and the monk within. She has served as a faculty at Villanova University, Prescott College, and Grinnell College. Dedicated to a vision of theological openness and spiritual nonviolence, her work has won praise for its wisdom, eloquence, and mystical insight and is considered to be a major contribution to new traditions of mystical wisdom for the 21st century. Follow Beverly's work at https://beverlylanzetta.net/.

Peter Russell is a leading thinker on consciousness and contemporary spirituality. He coined the term "global brain" with his 1980s bestseller of the same name in which he predicted the internet and the impact it would have on humanity. He is the author of twelve other books, including *Waking Up in Time, From Science to God*, and his most recent, *Letting Go of Nothing: Relax Your Mind and Discover the Wonder of Your True Nature*. He studied theoretical physics, experimental psychology, and computer science at the University of Cambridge, and meditation and eastern philosophy in India. In the 1980s he pioneered the introduction of personal growth programs to corporations. His mission is to distill the essential wisdom of human consciousness found in the world's various spiritual traditions, and to disseminate their teachings on self-liberation in contemporary and compelling ways. Follows Peter's work at https://www.peterrussell.com/index.php.

Ervin Laszlo is a philosopher and systems scientist. The author, co-author, or editor of 106 books that have appeared in twenty-five languages, he has written over 400 articles and research papers. The subject of the one-hour PBS special titled "Life of a Modern-Day Genius," Laszlo is the founder and president of the international think tank, The Club of Budapest, and of the prestigious Laszlo Institute of New Paradigm Research. The recipient of various honors and awards, including honorary PhDs from the United States, Canada, Finland, and Hungary, Laszlo received the Goi Award, the Japan Peace Prize in 2001, the Assisi Mandir of Peace Prize in 2006, and was nominated for the Nobel Peace Prize in 2004 and 2005. He lives in the Tuscan hills of the Mediterranean coast of Italy. Follow Ervin's work at https://ervinlaszlobooks.com/ and https://thelaszloinstitute.com/.

Sheri D. Kling is director of Process and Faith and the John Cobb Legacy Fund in Claremont, California. She is also a theologian, teacher, and songwriter who draws from wisdom and mystical traditions, relational worldviews, depth psychology, and the intersection of spirituality and science to help people find meaning, belonging, and transformation. She is a faculty member of the Haden Institute, adjunct faculty with Claremont School of Theology, and author of *A Process Spirituality: Christian and Transreligious Resources for Transformation*. She regularly delivers dynamic "Music & Message" presentations to groups, and offers courses, concerts, and spiritual retreats. She lives in Bradenton, Florida and may be found online at sherikling.com.

Rupert Spira is a teacher and practitioner of nonduality. At the age of seventeen he learned to meditate, and began a twenty-year period of study and practice in the classical Advaita Vedanta tradition under the guidance of Dr. Francis Roles and Shantananda Saraswati, the Shankaracharya of the north of India. During this time, he immersed himself in the teachings of P.D. Ouspensky, Krishnamurti, Rumi, Ramana Maharshi, Nisargadatta, and Robert Adams, until he met his teacher, Francis Lucille, in 1997. Francis introduced Rupert to the Direct Path teachings of Atmananda Krishnamenon, the Tantric tradition of Kashmir Shaivism (which he had received from his teacher, Jean Klein), and, more importantly, directly indicated to him the true nature of experience. Rupert lives in Britain and holds regular meetings and retreats in Europe and the U.S. Follow Rupert's work at https://rupertspira.com/.

Kabir Helminski is co-director and co-founder with his wife Camille Helminski of The Threshold Society, a nonprofit educational foundation that has developed programs to provide a structure for practice and study within Sufism and spiritual psychology. He is a shaikh of the Mevlevi Order of Sufis, which traces its inspiration to Jelaluddin Rumi. He began his Mevlevi training as a student of the late Shaikh Suleyman Loras. In 1990, he was subsequently appointed a shaikh by the late Dr. Celaleddin Celebi of Istanbul, Turkey, head of the Mevlevi Tariqa (Order) and twenty-first generation descendant of Mevlâna Jalâluddîn Rumi. Under

Kabir's direction, The Mevlevi Order is working to apply traditional Sufi principles to the conditions of contemporary life. Follow Kabir's work at https://sufism.org/.

Jude Currivan is a cosmologist, planetary healer, futurist, author, previously one of the most senior business women in Britain and co-founder of WholeWorld-View. Having grown up as the daughter of a coal miner in the north of England, she has since journeyed to more than eighty countries around the world, and for the last twenty-five years has lived in the sacred landscape of Avebury. She has experienced multidimensional realities since early childhood and worked with the wisdom keepers, both incarnate and discarnate, of many traditions. Jude integrates leading edge science, research into consciousness and universal wisdom teachings into a wholistic world-view. This underpins her work, which aims to enable transformational and emergent resolutions to our collective planetary issues, raise awareness, and empower fundamental change and sustainable solutions to global problems. She holds a PhD in Archaeology from the University of Reading where she researched ancient cosmologies, and a MA in Physics from Oxford University where she specializing in cosmology and quantum physics. She is the author of seven non-fiction books translated into sixteen languages. Follow Jude's work at https://www.judecurrivan.com/.

Karen Johnson is the co-developer of the Diamond Approach as it is taught in the Ridhwan School today, having worked alongside Hameed Ali (A. H. Almaas) for the last forty years. Karen was trained in art and dance and began the journey into the spiritual universe at fourteen years old with the guidance of her parents. First, she was introduced to yoga and meditation, and then learned about other forms of spiritual practice, which allowed her to develop her innate paranormal capacities. After attending California College of Arts and Crafts, she befriended Hameed Ali, and with him began a new trajectory into the secrets of the universe of Being, which became the Diamond Approach. Karen also received an

MA in psychology John F. Kennedy University in 1990. She continues to venture into new explorations of the endless realms of our indeterminant miraculous Nature. She is the author of *The Jeweled Path: The Biography of the Diamond Approach to Inner Self-Realization*, and co-author with A.H. Almaas of *The Power of Divine Eros*. Learn more about the Diamond Approach at https://www.diamondapproach.org/.

Hameed Ali (A.H. Almaas) was born in Kuwait in 1944. At the age of eighteen, he moved to the U.S. to study at the University of California in Berkeley. Hameed was working on his PhD in physics when he reached a turning point in his life and destiny that led him to inquire into the psychological and spiritual aspects of human nature rather than the physical nature of the universe. He left the academic world to pursue an in-depth journey of inner discovery, applying his scientific precision and discipline to personal, experiential research. This included study with different teachers in different modalities, extensive reading, and continuous study of his own consciousness in an effort to understand the essential nature of human experience and reality in general. Hameed's process of exploration led to the creation of the Ridhwan School and, with Karen Johnson, resulted in the founding of the Diamond Approach. He is the author of many books. Learn more about the Diamond Approach at https://www.diamondapproach.org/.

Jay McDaniel is an American philosopher and theologian. He specializes in Buddhism, Whiteheadian process philosophy and process theology, constructive theology, ecotheology, interfaith dialogue, and spirituality in an age of consumerism. In addition to publishing numerous books and articles, McDaniel is an active voice for process philosophy and theology on social media. He runs a popular blog called Open Horizons to offer ideas that might help people create multi-cultural, interfaith communities that are creative, compassionate, participatory, ecologically wise, and spiritually enjoyable. He's also a consultant for the China Project of the Center for Process Studies and a member of the advisory board of the Institute for Postmodern Development of China. He earned a BA in English literature and philosophy from Vanderbilt University and a PhD in philosophy of religion and theology from Claremont Graduate University. Follow Jay's work at https://www.openhorizons.org/.

Amit Goswami is a theoretical quantum physicist and renegade scientist who ventures into the domain of the spiritual in an attempt to interpret the seemingly inexplicable findings of curious experiments and validate intuitions about the existence of a spiritual dimension of life. A prolific writer, teacher, and visionary, Amit developed a theory of reincarnation and integrated conventional and alternative medicine within the new quantum science of health. Among his discoveries are the quantum theory of the creative process, the theory of quantum evolution, and the theory of quantum economics that extends Adam's Smith's capitalism into a workable paradigm for the twenty-first century. In 2009, he started a movement called "quantum activism," now gaining ground in North and South America, southern and eastern Europe, and India. In 2018, together with his collaborators, he established Quantum Activism Vishwalayam, an institution of transformative education in India, based on quantum science and the primacy of consciousness. This program offers masters and PhD programs in the quantum science of health, prosperity, and happiness under the auspices of University of Technology, Jaipur. Amit is the author of numerous books including most recently, *Quantum Spirituality* with Valentina Onisor. Follow Amit's work at https://www.amitgoswami.org/.

Becca Tarnas is a scholar, artist, counseling astrologer, and editor of *Archai: The Journal of Archetypal Cosmology*. She received her PhD in philosophy and religion at the California Institute of Integral Studies (CIIS) in San Francisco. Her dissertation was titled, The Back of Beyond: The Red Books of C.G. Jung and J.R.R. Tolkien. She now teaches at both Pacifica Graduate Institute and CIIS, as well as several other online education platforms. She is the author of *Journey to the Imaginal Realm: A*

Reader's Guide to J.R.R. Tolkien's The Lord of the Rings. Follow Becca's work at https://beccatarnas.com/.

Christopher M. Bache is professor emeritus in the department of philosophy and religious studies at Youngstown State University, where he taught for thirty-three years. A fellow at the Institute of Noetic Sciences, he is also adjunct faculty at California Institute of Integral Studies, and on the advisory board for Grof Transpersonal Training and the Grof Foundation. An award-winning teacher and international speaker, he is the author of three books including *LSD and the Mind of the Universe*, which meticulously documents his insights from seventy-three high-dose LSD sessions conducted over the course of twenty years. Follow Chris' work at https://chrisbache.com/.

Raymond Moody coined the term "near-death experience" in his *New York Times* bestselling book, *Life After Life.* He has given thousands of presentations on near-death and shared-death experiences to audiences around the world, and he has published several bestselling books. He holds a PhD in philosophy from the University of Virginia, a PhD in psychology from the University of West Georgia, and an MD in psychiatry from the Medical College of Georgia. He lives near Birmingham, Alabama. Follow Raymond's work at https://www.lifeafterlife.com/.